REVIVAL in WALES

the GREAT REVIVAL *in* WALES

S.B. Shaw

CHRISTIAN LIFE BOOKS

THE PUBLISHING ARM OF RIVER OF REVIVAL MINISTRIES, INC.

PENSACOLA, FL 32516

CHRISTIAN LIFE BOOKS
P.O. BOX 36355
PENSACOLA, FLORIDA 32516

DRLARRYMARTIN.COM
AZUSASTREET.ORG
PENTECOSTALGOLD.COM
JESUS-IS-THE-ANSWER.COM

mail@drlarrymartin.org

Dedication

This reprint is dedicated to the members of Moriah Chapel who through their faithfulness keep the fire burning and the memories of revival alive.

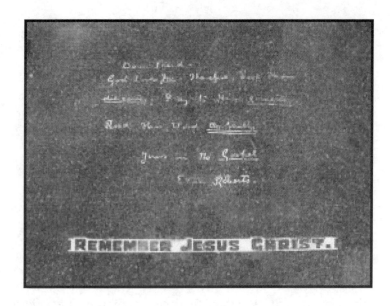

The words of Evan Roberts from a memorial marker at Moriah Chapel:

Dear Friend—

God loves you. Therefore, seek Him diligently; pray to Him earnestly; Read His word continually.

Yours in the service

Evan Roberts

Remember Jesus Christ

CONTENTS

LIST OF PHOTOGRAPHS

A YOUNG
EVAN ROBERTS

FOREWORD

On October 22, 1996, God wonderfully changed my life. In the midst of Holy Ghost revival in Miami, Oklahoma, He intervened and changed me forever. Since that night, my passion has been revival.

Constantly, I am in revival, praying for revival, studying past revivals, and reading or writing about revival. **Christian Life Books** is the visible manifestation of our desire to document history's greatest revivals through original works and reprinted classics.

My primary interest has been early Pentecostal revivals, especially the Azusa Street Revival that started in Los Angeles, California in 1906. That revival, however, like all others, did not start in a vacuum. It was in many ways connected to the revival in Wales.

Joseph Smale, pastor of First Baptist Church in Los Angeles, made a pilgrimage to Wales to meet

Evan Roberts and witness the revival first hand. Upon his return, daily prayer meetings commenced in the church he pastored. The seasons of prayer lasted more than three months and prepared many for the coming visitation of God's Holy Spirit.

In 1905, the noted English preacher, F. B. Meyers held meetings in Los Angeles. He, too, spoke sympathetically about the move of God in Wales. A local evangelist, Frank Bartleman said Meyers' preaching stirred his soul "to its depths."

At the same time, Bartleman began corresponding with Roberts about the Welsh revival. Roberts wrote, "Congregate the people who are willing to make a total surrender. Pray and wait. Believe God's promises. Hold daily meetings. May God bless you is my earnest prayer." Bartleman distributed a tract about the Welsh revival written by G. Campbell Morgan and copies of this book, *The Great Revival in Wales*. The book made its impact on Los Angeles and soon the city was experiencing a similar move of God.

Christian Life Books re-releases this classic with the prayer that it will create the same kind of hunger today and that wherever it is read it will fan the flames of revival.

The book is reprinted almost exactly as it was first written. Some punctuation and spelling have been changed to modernize the work and editorial comments have been added to explain some colloquialisms. Only one word in the original text was replaced and only because it had taken on a vulgar meaning since Shaw's original was published.

In the original, Shaw reprinted a chapter from a book on the revival in Ireland in 1859. In my opinion, it did not add to the work and I have chosen not to include it.

Pastor Peter Yeoman hosted me and a group from Brownsville Revival School of Ministry at his church in Swansea, Wales and was gracious enough to arrange a tour of Moriah Chapel. His kindness, and the hospitality of the precious members of Moriah Chapel, will be remembered forever.

Larry E. Martin, D.Min.
Pensacola, Florida

S. B. SHAW
1854-1941
A METHODIST-EPISCOPAL MINSTER,
EDITOR OF
THE MICHIGAN HOLINESS RECORD
AND AUTHOR OF THIS BOOK.

PREFATORY NOTE

For years many of God's elect have been led out in the Spirit to cry unto Him day and night for a widespread, heaven-born revival of pure and undefiled religion—for a worldwide revival of Pentecostal power and glory, and have had the assurance of victory. Never before have we known such faith and prayer among those who live in close communion with God, and now all can see that the spirit of faith and desire and expectancy is deepening and spreading, and in many places glorious revivals are already in progress. Speaking of this desire and of the burden of prayer resting upon her, one sister writes: "I have been in an agony of soul for weeks. It seems at times as if it would almost take my life;" and this is the language of our own and many other hearts.

Several National Convocations of Prayer have been held in different parts of our own land, and at every one God has granted to His own, very much of the spirit of prayer and intercession. Many have spent whole nights weeping and crying to God to revive His work, knowing in their own inmost souls the groanings of the Spirit that could not be uttered. Nor has the spirit of prayer been confined to any one class, or place, or denomination.

That God is leading out His saints, and by His own right hand of power preparing the way for a general outpouring of His Spirit in this as in other lands, is blessedly manifest.

To aid in this work, we have gathered together these various reports of the gracious and glorious revival now going on in Wales, believing that everywhere these reports go, God can use them to stir up other hearts to increase faith and prayer, and so hasten the coming of the glorious day for which we watch and pray.

God help us all to lay hold upon God, and to "give Him no rest" "till He make Jerusalem a praise in the earth!"

Yours for the faith once delivered to the saints,

S.B. Shaw

Chicago, Ill., April, 1905

THE REVIVAL IN WALES

Wales is in the throes and ecstasies of the most remarkable religious revival it has ever known. It is nothing less than a "moral revolution." The last great movement of the kind which swept over the land was in the years 1859-60, a period that was memorably fruitful for the cause of Christ throughout the kingdom generally, notably in the north of Ireland. There are many still living in Wales who speak of those "good old times" with pardonable pride and thankfulness. They are the "fathers and mothers in Israel" today. I have heard some of these testifying in recent meetings in the Rhondda Valley. With one consent they declare that even that remarkable "season of refreshing from the presence of the Lord"—which witnessed thousands brought to decision for Christ—pales before the glory of this modern Pentecost.

Already, in five or six weeks, the fire has spread to six or seven counties, and bids fair to find its way as did Daniel Rowlands, of Llangeitho, that great evangelist of the eighteenth century—"into every parish in Wales, from Cardiff to Holyhead, and from Presteign to St. David's." What has largely contributed to the rapidity of the movement is the widespread publicity given to it in the press—both secular and religious. Every day for weeks past the *South Wales Daily News* and the *Western Mail,* the two leading dailies in South Wales, have devoted three or four columns to reports of it. The evening papers, too, are full of it. Formerly, as someone has observed, they devoted whole columns to sport, and a paltry paragraph or two to anything concerning the kingdom of Christ. Now it is the other way about. What everybody is talking about, and anxious to hear about, in South Wales, is "the revival," and the proprietors of the press are not at all slack in catering for the public taste.

The converts already number many thousands. Mr. Evan Roberts calculates that in the mining valleys of South Wales alone—that southeastern corner of the principality which is well marked on any railway map—there have been at least 10,000 conversions. And if we add to this the harvest gleaned in various other places north and south, the number cannot be far short of 20,000. For, be it understood there are many districts in the principality where a mighty work is going on, and where meetings are held almost day and night, of which no reports have been forthcoming in the press. The counties of Carmarthen and Cardigan, *e.g.,* as also many places in North Wales, are all astir and sharing in the general blessing. The movement has penetrated into some of the remotest corners of the principality, and many a distant lonely valley is echoing the glad music of salvation. Figures, of course, are not everything; but for Wales these figures are astonishing, when it is borne in mind that they represent net additions to the membership of the churches which already numbered upon their books about one half of the entire population of the country, and that the margin left for aggression, therefore, was nothing like as large as would be the case, say, in England. Moreover, the churches themselves have experienced a great quickening, and many, both ministers and people, have testified to a new joy and power, and to receiving a baptism of the Holy Spirit.

The question is frequently asked, "How and where did the revival originate?" Recent as it is, its human and historical origin seems to baffle discovery. But, truth to tell, there is not much anxiety on that score. Everybody seems to be so interested in its progress as not to be troubled about its origin." But it has been definitely ascertained that for some time previously there was a yearning in the heart of many devout and godly people for such an awakening, and amongst the faithful an expectation of it. For, religious as Wales was considered to be—with its love of the Bible, the sanctuary, sacred song, and the Sabbath school there were ominous "signs of the times" which made the faithful watchers on Zion's hilltops tremble, and drove them to their knees in earnest prayer. Prayer soon became prophecy. Only three months ago one of the saintliest of Welsh preachers publicly proclaimed from the pulpit his absolute conviction "that a mighty outpouring of the Spirit was at hand, and that marvelous times would follow." Well—*the marvelous has happened*—and happened in unexpected fashion. For weeks past, meetings have been going on in various parts of the country, and, in numerous instances, have been protracted into the small hours of the morning. The extraordinary thing about these meetings is their unconventional character. There is no organization, no program, no presenter, no presiding elder! Everything is left to the direction of the Holy Spirit. Preaching, in the usual acceptation of the word, has, for the time being, been entirely discarded, and is superseded by singing, prayer, and general testimony.

Methodist Recorder

Evan Roberts' Call from God

EVAN ROBERTS

THE WELSH REVIVAL AND THE REMARKABLE LEADER WHO HAS SPRUNG FROM THE COLLIER TO THE WORLD'S LIMELIGHT

A wonderful revival is sweeping over Wales. The whole country, from the city to the colliery (coal mine. Ed.) underground, is aflame with gospel glory. Police courts are hardly necessary, public houses are being deserted, old debts are being paid to satisfy awakened consciences and definite and unmistakable answers to prayer are recorded.

The leader in this great religious movement is a young man twenty-six years of age, Evan Roberts. He was a collier boy, then an apprentice in a forge, then a student for the ministry. But all his life he has yearned to preach the gospel. He is no orator. He is not widely read. The only book he knows from cover to cover is the Bible. He has in his possession a Bible which he values above anything else he has belonging to him. It is a Bible slightly scorched in a colliery explosion. When the evangelist was working in a colliery, he used to take his Bible with him, and while at work would put it away in some convenient hole or nook near his working place, ready to his hand when he could snatch a moment or two to scan its beloved pages. A serious explosion occurred one day. The future Welsh revivalist escaped practically unhurt, but the leaves of his Bible were scorched by the fiery blast. "Evan Roberts' scorched Bible" is a familiar phrase among his friends.

Little more than a month ago Evan Roberts was unknown, studying for one of the Welsh colleges at Newcastle-Emlyn, so as to prepare for the Calvinistic Methodist ministry. Then came the summons, and he obeyed. He insists that he has been called to his present work by the direct guidance of the Holy Ghost. At once, without question and without hesitation, he was accepted by the people. Wherever he went hearts were set aflame with the love of God.

Here is a vivid report of one of his meetings, given by a newspaper representative, "The scene was almost indescribable. Tier upon tier of men and women filled every inch of space. Those who could not gain admittance stood outside and listened at the doors. Others rushed to the windows, where almost every word was audible. When, at seven o'clock, the service began, quite 2,000 people must have been present. The enthusiasm was unbounded. Women sang and shouted till the perspiration ran down their faces, and men jumped up one after the other to testify. One told in quivering accents the story of a drunken life. A working collier spoke like a practiced orator, and one can imagine what a note the testimony of a converted gypsy woman struck when, dressed in her best, she told of her reformation and repentance. At ten o'clock the meeting had lost none of its ardor. Prayer after prayer went up from those Welsh hearts with almost dreary persistence. Time and again the four ministers who stood in the pulpit attempted to start a hymn but it was all in vain. The revival has taken hold of the people, and even Mr. Roberts cannot hold it in check. His latest convert is a policeman, who, after complaining that the people had gone mad after religion, so that there was nothing to do, went to see for himself, and bursting into tears, confessed the error of his way and repented."

Meetings such as this are being repeated every day, and the enthusiasm is still spreading. While there has been no organization, no elaborate preparation for this mission, in the ordinary sense of the word, there is a strong belief that it is the direct result of earnest prayer. A prominent member of a Newport Baptist church, who has followed the movement with close interest and deep thankfulness, declared the other day the revival was the result of the praying by the young women who had been engaged in it for some months. Evan Roberts had, he said, been praying for thirteen months for that wave to come, and he related how the young man was turned out of his lodgings by his landlady, who thought that in his enthusiasm he was possessed or somewhat mad. He spent hours praying and preaching in his rooms, until the lady became afraid of him, and asked him to leave.

It may be observed that the dominant note of the revival is prayer and praise. Another striking fact is the joyousness and radiant happiness of the evangelist. It has been remarked that the very essence of his campaign is mirth (rejoicing. Ed.). To the rank and file of the church ministers this is his most incomprehensible phase. They have always regarded religion as something iron bound, severe, even terrible. Evan Roberts smiles when he prays, laughs when he preaches. "Ah, it is a grand life," he cries. "I am happy, so happy that I could walk on the air. Tired? Never! God has made me strong. He has given me courage."

He is a leader who preaches victory, and shows how it may be won—victory over the dull depression and gloomy doubt of our time. Is it surprising that followers flock in thousands to his banner? It has long been felt in Wales, as elsewhere, that the time was ripe for a great religious revival. As the Rev. H. M. Hughes, a Congregational minister in Cardiff, recently pointed out, all efforts, movements, and organizations did not stem the flood of evil or stop the growth of pleasure seeking and mammon worship. A generation had risen that had not seen the arm of God working as it had done in 1849 and 1859.

Now, to all appearances, the revival has arrived, and it has many of the marks of previous great awakenings. Strong men are held in its grip; the Spirit of God stirs to their very depths whole neighborhoods and districts. There is a tumult of emotion, an overpowering influence, and a conviction of sin that can only be attributed to Divine agency. Personal eloquence, magnetism, fervor, or mental power do not account for it. The only explanation is the one which the evangelist gives—it is all of God. And it has already done infinite good in places far away from its immediate locality. Men are everywhere thinking, talking, discussing religious topics, and at last God, Christ, and the soul have to some degree come to their own. This is all gain. The revival seems to work especially among young people. Its form, which is that of prayer, praise, and personal testimony, and its absence of method, make it the most methodical expression of the emotions of young hearts aflame with the love of God.

The Ram's Horn

REPORT BY MRS. BAXTER

This mighty movement must be seen to be understood. A sense of awe came over me again and again as in a large chapel, on a weekday afternoon; I saw a large, deep gallery surrounding the chapel literally packed with men. They were manly, intensely earnest faces, not looking around or talking one to the other, but with one consent utterly taken up with God. The body of the chapel was also crowded with men and women of all classes, with but one purpose—*to meet God.*

There was no opening of the meeting; the hearts were full, and burst with prayer and praise to a God felt to be in our midst. One gentleman who had come from Oxford to see the work, said, "These men are not praying to be heard of man; it doesn't matter to them what people think of them; they are thinking about the answer, not about the hearers;" and it was true. At times a wave of power, without any human instrumentality, or anything external to cause it, would sweep over the mass of the people, and spontaneously almost the whole company would pray aloud, no one heeding the other, and without the slightest confusion. Every one was absorbed with God; but in the midst of it, no one dealing with them, a man here, a woman there, would yield to God, and in a few minutes stand up and give praise that they had found the Lord. Sometimes singing and prayer would go on together, but there was no real confusion—the praying was not to man, and the singing was not to man. But such singing is rarely to be heard. It was perfect time and perfect harmony; often the same hymn (never given out, but started spontaneously), sung in English and in Welsh at the same time, and sung over and over, until it penetrated. There was no organ, nor need for one; when men—for the women were too few to make much impression—sing unto the Lord in this way, an organ is out of place. It was heart-singing, "singing with melody in your heart to the Lord" (Eph. 5:19).

I was present at three meetings in which Mr. Evan Roberts was not present, nor yet either of the young lady singers who help in some of the meetings. But God was there; and though Mr. Roberts was expected in the afternoon, not a murmur of disappointment was expressed—God was present, and He satisfied. In two morning meetings where I had the privilege to be, the same Spirit reigned; as the people gathered, the prayers and hymns burst forth—no one led but the Spirit Himself. One and another entered the place, knelt down, and in a few minutes an intense prayer, or as intense a chorus or verse of a hymn was sung, or a text of Scripture or a chapter read—but all in the most perfect harmony and intensity. Mr. Roberts himself is as simple and natural as a child; he comes into the meetings, and in no way interferes with what is going on, and no one stops in prayer, singing, or testimony because he appears. He waits until there is a moment's pause, and then speaks a few strong, simple words, with no apparent oratory, but an intensity which calls forth earnest responses from the congregation. Sometimes he asks a question, and they answer. He opens the Bible, but there is too much singing at the moment, and he quietly closes it, sits down out of sight, and remains in silent prayer. He has a real belief in the leading of the Holy Spirit, and knows how to wait *on* the Lord and wait *for* the Lord.

The proceedings were mostly in Welsh, but a kind man of God, or some kind sister, would translate for me, or put me in the way of understanding what was going on. There was prayer made in a little group close to me for a man in the gallery; it was quiet—a group kneeling while others were standing and singing around. Shortly that one in the gallery, knowing nothing of the prayer; got up and said he was saved. In the singing of the lady revivalists there is much power, and the same following of the Spirit. No one announces them; they simply await the opportunity. This is indeed the mighty hand of God.

Man is at a discount. "The Lord alone shall be exalted in that day." We are reminded of that day when the Holy Spirit came down upon the hundred and twenty on the Day of Pentecost. "And they were all filled with the Holy Ghost, and began to speak with other tongues, as the Spirit gave them utterance." No intellectual treatises, no trained choirs needed, when God the Holy Ghost can find yielded, obedient hearts to occupy, and tongues through which to speak. Drunkenness, swearing, stealing, quarreling, flee before the presence of the Lord in His people. What is the secret of this movement? On man's part, believing, persevering prayer; on God's part, the promised answer.

The Eleventh Hour

THE REVIVAL IN THE WEST—STRIKING STORIES AND INCIDENTS
"THE WASH-DAY OF THE LORD"
BY REV. T. FERRIER HULME, M. A.

The last issue of *The Methodist Times* has brought me much correspondence, revealing the widespread interest in the revival. Perhaps the most touching and suggestive letter is from a probationer, who says: "Yesterday my quarterly meeting very kindly offered to send me to the scene of the revival for a week in view of the missions I am undertaking here. Like you, I believe the revival is a manifestation of God, and I look forward to my visit as a supreme opportunity for getting a personal blessing, and trust

I may return, like one of Samson's foxes, to 'burn the world out with the sweet gift of fire.' What a blessed awakening awaits England if our people will realize the infinite possibilities of prayer and the unspent resources of God." It is almost impossible to exaggerate the demand for well-authenticated news. Last week a reporter, having heard that a journalist of worldwide renown had been spending Sunday at Maerdy, and was staying in Cardiff on the Monday night, telephoned from a distant town to one hotel after another till he found him, and was then informed he had gone to bed. "Never mind, tell him I must speak to him now." The victim was dragged from his bed to the telephone, only, to be asked, "What do you think of the revival?"

Not the least interesting part of one's experience is the journey thither. At every wayside station you pick up pilgrims, many of them ministers, and from one end of the train to the other you have revival talk and song. Those who know Wales know how the denominations are duplicated, and how pronounced and even bitter have been denominational jealousies, especially in the small towns. For the time being all these distinctions are forgotten. You find yourself talking to a brother minister, and in a few moments you are rejoicing with him in the *Pentecostal power that has come* upon his church and neighborhood. You don't know to what sect he belongs, and you don't care, and when you have left him you awake to the discovery that whilst you have asked him many things it has not occurred to you to ask him that. Like you, he is anxious that the Spirit may be glorified and the community regenerated, and that is enough to satisfy your heart. The movement is as undenominational as the air, but the results are not. People are joining the churches by scores and hundreds. In many cases the membership is doubled. This is as it should be.

The spontaneity of the work is glorious, and the lack of organization is most refreshing. It is all so novel, and so contradictory to what we are accustomed to regard as essential. There is no creaking of the machinery. The stir is caused by the blowing of the wind—the breath of Heaven. Where all is so black and grimy, and the one cry is for cleansing, we all felt we could understand the fervent exclamation of the simple-hearted collier, "Lord, this is Thy wash-day," and forgive the familiarity. The absence of advertising posters and window bills causes no confusion. Everything is advertised by living witnesses and signs following. You walk, as I did, into a town of 14,000 inhabitants, while there are at least twenty chapels, and you ask the first person you meet, "Where is the meeting?" and he tells you. The only advertisement I have seen was in another district, and was the most significant thing of the kind I have known in these modern days. As I walked down the streets of Aberfau and Merthyr Vale last week I read in the shop window:

Merthyr Vale Chamber of Trade
REVIVAL MEETINGS
This Establishment will be
CLOSED
Thursday, December 15,
Owing to the visit of Mr. Evan Roberts

They told me the same applied on that day to the two pits (mines. Ed.) in the neighborhood. On the previous day I saw what I have often seen in Roman Catholic countries, but never before in this

Protestant land. Seven chapels were open throughout the day for prayer and worship, and people walked in and came out, as they felt inclined during those continuous services. Four of those chapels were crowded and two of them were densely packed. I got into the schoolroom of one, and found the people standing rows deep, but I could not get near the chapel door. Presently the school door was locked, but it made no difference. People opened the window and came through in orderly fashion till every vacant square foot was utilized. I said, "If there's a way in there's a way out," and out I shot and adjourned to one of the seven open sanctuaries where a hearty meeting was conducting itself hour after hour without let or hindrance, in which I was soon moved to take part. These two small townships of Aberfau and Merthyr Vale in this narrow valley are on opposite slopes, separated only by the Taff. The united population is about 9,000. There are four public houses (pubs, taverns. Ed.), three of which are tied houses. Throughout the day they are in a state of semi-desertion. The coffee tavern is besieged at all hours, and the swarming visitors, who cannot get in, satisfy their hunger by purchases at the grocer's and fruiterer's. For beds they flee to other towns, and take what they can get. I interviewed the landlady of one of the "pubs," who told me she was against the revival, and—*preferred ordinary religion.*

I asked her why, and she said that on one night the enthusiasts gathered outside her establishment, and sang heartily, and then prayed fervently that God would have mercy on the prodigals inside— and her customers were not prodigals, and were not likely to be.

As soon as the policeman could release himself from the society of the barmaid, standing at the door of the largest and noisiest public house in the center of the town, I interviewed him. He assured me that foul language and drunkenness had greatly diminished, and that his own duties (and evidently the barmaid's) were considerably lightened. He added, "The barmaid has just told me that the publican and his wife have gone to the service, and that is a new thing for them." "Is there much diminution in his receipts?" I asked. "Oh, yes; but he puts it down to the approach of Christmas, and to the fact that the colliers are saving their wages for the time of feasting—but others know differently," he remarked with significant emphasis. On inquiry of the trade's people, they also admitted that their sales were not what they should be. "How is that?" "Well, you see, people are paying their debts and settling old scores. It will be all the better for us in a little while."

I talked also to pitmen (miners. Ed.) who had the same story to tell of amendment and reformation. Having obtained these facts from the business and trading community, I asked the local ministers what reports they had to give. I found that for three weeks previous to the visit of Evan Roberts they had conducted among themselves mission services, that hundreds had professed conversion, and that all the churches had been daily gladdened by the addition of those who were being saved.

"What sort of converts are they?" I asked. "Mostly backsliders," said a man in the street. When a church is not aggressive it consoles itself by saying that it is just about holding its own. What a false notion! "Mostly backsliders," tells another tale.

It seems to me that God has now given to His church in Wales an advantage over the enemy similar to that which the Japanese have acquired over the Russians by the capture of 203 Metre Hill. God's people are now sweeping these Welsh hills and valleys with a searching fire, that is devastating the strongholds of sin, and in some instances is leading to almost wholesale capture. Evan Roberts did not arrive that day till five o'clock, when services had been in progress for about seven hours. I did not see him. I did not attempt to see him. I had my turn previously, and I was glad to be of some service in chapels that he could not visit. His coming constituted a great field day. But, *the victory had been gained* in the previous weeks, and the attack will still be renewed in the days to come, and there will be further fighting all along the line. The fire is not spent, and the ammunition is not low.

I always feel that I want to join in the *Diolch Iddo* (a popular Welsh song of praise. Ed.) when I see the crowds of men, and especially of young men, at these services. There is sure to be a certain amount of reaction in the days to come, judging by past history, but thousands of these men have got a blessing they will never lose, and an inspiration that will make them grand fishers of men. It will give to us all renewed faith in prayer, for this is emphatically a praying revival. Evan Roberts told me that prayer became so passionate and mighty at Caerphilly that at midnight a number of men formed themselves into a praying "Get-them-out-of-bed brigade," and in an hour or two three of the sinners prayed for became so miserable in bed that they dressed hurriedly and came on to the service and yielded to Christ there and then. After I have seen over and over again the complete abandonment with which men give themselves up to pleading, as if they were totally unconscious of any presence but that of Christ, and were quite unaffected by anything or anybody else, I can easily believe it. Even when I could not understand a single word I have been indescribably moved. How, then, must it be with the Father who knows all and loves all? Humanity in Wales is as frail as it is elsewhere, but I have had a new lesson in this text, "The Spirit also helpeth our infirmity."

I have heard a young Russian offer his first prayer in English, and a young Welshman give his first testimony in English. He was the young man who said in broken English, "When I was a boy and went to the seaside to bathe, and saw a big wave coming along, I just ducked. Friends, a big tidal wave is sweeping along this valley. *Be sure you duck,* and then you'll get the baptism."

That, I suppose, is the preliminary stage, but if people will then proceed to plunge and to swim, they will be able to take full advantage of this glorious tide, for, as Ezekiel says, "The waters were risen, waters to swim in, a river that could not be passed through."

Some people take exception to this revival because there are those who declare they see visions and hear voices. Of these you hear but little. You often hear prayer for illumination, as when a woman exclaimed, "May we draw up the blinds of the soul, and let in the light!" There is much figurative language like that in prayer which always evokes response. In these services everything seems to gain by spontaneity of feeling and expression.

I heard what the *Daily News* representative aptly termed, "The Tabloid Sermon," by a young American, on Isa. 1:18. The people listened gladly to the text, but when he proceeded to say, "There are five 'C's' in this verse, and I want you to see these five 'C's'—the call, conviction, communion, cleansing, and confession," some of them *didn't* see it, and wearied before he got to fifthly. However, they managed to keep fairly still, and then roused themselves and us by one of their glorious songs. We felt that such ingenuity was a poor substitute for spontaneity.

Extraordinary incidents are as numerous as ever. At Cardiff a young man, who had been lost to his parents for three years, turned up at the very service where his father (a county magistrate) and his mother were praying for him. His father knelt at his side to help him to Jesus, but the son did not recognize him till they both rose to give praise! They then went together to find the mother, who in another part of the chapel was earnestly praying for her lost boy, and who was totally oblivious of anything and any one around her. The scene was indescribably pathetic (emotional. Ed.), and the joy of all was ecstatic.

At one of Evan Roberts's meetings a young man told how he spent his early years at Oxford in training for a monk. He ran away to sea, and was absent for twelve years. He settled in business in Wales, and spent all his leisure in drinking clubs and similar resorts. A month ago, when on his way to his club, he was pressed to go to chapel by a friend. He absolutely refused, but on repeated pressure by his friend he said, "I'll toss for it. Heads, I go to the chapel;

tails, I go to the club." He tossed, and it came heads. He went to the chapel, and he was then and there converted. This was a man well known in his own town.

In the Coegnant Colliery 200 hauliers and miners joined in prayer and praise. Those who desired to confess Christ were asked to signify the fact by holding their lamps aloft. Lamps went up by the score.

And so I might go on, but perhaps I cannot do better than give a somewhat free translation by Mr. Thomas of some of the sweetest songs of the revival. The three verses selected are good specimens of what you repeatedly hear sung with such fervor:

(1) "*Gwaed y Groes,*" &c.
Jesus Christ lifts up the weary,
With a smile divinely sweet;
Jesus Christ brings down the mighty,
Kneeling, trembling at His feet.
Blessed Savior,
Send a breeze from Calvary!

(2) "*Dyma Geidwad*" &c.
Here's a Savior for the fallen,
Here's a Healer for us all.
Here is One who loves forgiving
Sinners, damaged by the fall.
Praise Thee, Jesus,
Ever, for remembering me!

(3) "'R *Hwn Sy'n Gyru'r mellt Hedeg,*'" &c.
Thou that sendest forth the lightning,
Thou that walkest on the sea,
Send the arrow of conviction

To these hearts, we pray to Thee.
Open wide our self-made prisons,
Send the firebrand from the flame,
Lift Thou up the weak and weary,
Teach the mute to praise Thy Name.

It is contrary to all precedent to have crowded revival services in the week before Christmas, but there are most hopeful signs that this outpouring, hitherto largely confined to the colliery districts, will descend copiously upon such important centers as Newport and Cardiff. Already we hear of many remarkable conversions in some of the town churches, and of well-attended prayer meetings in the large business houses; and when the Christmas holidays are over, and the New Year begins, we shall most probably be rejoicing over much more stirring scenes.

IT SPREADS TO CWMBRAN

The revival which has broken out in South Wales does not remain in that part alone, and it does not require the presence of Evan Roberts to infuse the spirit of this revival into the Christian church. Extraordinary services have taken place in the Wesleyan Chapel at Cwmbran during the past fortnight. Cwmbran is situated exactly half way between Pontypool and Newport, and not far from the villages where the Spirit of God has been manifested so recently in such a remarkable way.

The first signs of the revival took place three Sundays ago, when after the sermon had been preached by the circuit lay agent on "Let me die the death of the righteous," he asked a few to testify for Christ, and one after another stood up and told what God had done for them. The last to testify was a brother who had been the greatest drunkard in the neighborhood. He told them how God led him to see the light when he was quite drunk (a statement for which the writer can vouch), and had now kept him for two years. His words took a firm hold of his companions, of whom no less than six have surrendered all to Christ during the past week, some of them being notorious drunkards.

The meetings have not been carried on in the usual way. They have been opened by prayer and reading, with short running comments by Mr. A. Brace, a young local preacher, varied with invitations to come to the front of any with whom God's Spirit was striving at the commencement and at different stages of the meeting.

What was and is remarkable right throughout the meetings is the spontaneity, on some occasions as many as half a dozen commencing to pray at one time, and continually brothers and sisters are on their feet to pray, waiting turns. One old brother attempted six times to pray, and each time was forestalled by some one.

It was a glorious sight to see sinners rising and coming to the penitent form (This was a bench-like seat at the front of the sanctuary, facing the congregation. Sinners would come to this "altar," kneel, and repent. Especially popular with the Salvation Army. Ed.) seeking forgiveness. Amongst those who have confessed Christ is a young man who had been brought up in the Roman Catholic faith. After the singing of Come to Jesus, the question was asked, who will come to Him now? A man got up and shouted, "I will," and then broke down. Then his wife came out to the penitent form, and all his children. Another case occurred during the singing of *Throw Out the Life Line*. A passerby who was drunk was so affected by the singing that he turned into the meeting. It was wonderful to see the change that took place in him before the meeting was over. He came forward and confessed Christ, and when the meeting closed he was a sober man. To describe all the incidents would take too much of your space. Never has the Spirit of God been felt in such a powerful manner before. Up to the present there have been sixty converts, and the meetings are to continue.

London Methodist Times
December 22

EFFECTS ON BRIDGEND

Rev. J. Sharp, Tondu, Glamorgan, writes, "This very gracious and spiritual wave of revival has reached the Bridgend Circuit. Last week, Mr. Dan Roberts and his helpers visited the Calvinistic Methodist Church, Aber Renfig, where united and overflow meetings were held. On Sunday all the churches were moved. At Tondu scenes were witnessed in the Sunday school as had not been seen before. The whole time was given up to praise and prayer. The classrooms were full of inquirers of all ages. The work was continued in the church in the evening, when several more volunteered for Christ. Monday brought the joyful news from Ogmore Vale, Maesteg, Bryncoch, Cefn, and Fountain, of similar results. Many who have long been prayed for have yielded; backsliders have come back, and many wonderful cases of conversion have taken place. The football field, the dance, and the dramatic entertainment have been given up, and other matters laid aside for the 'revival meetings.'"

A Meeting at Skewen

It was into the peculiarly sacred atmosphere created by an hour and a half of intensely spiritual worship that Evan Roberts came at two o'clock. They prayed and sang, and sang and prayed, as if nobody noticed him, and yet, of course, everybody had. This absorption in worship just suited him, and he was much impressed by the devout waiting upon God, instead of the mere waiting for the evangelist. The people were now singing, *Send the Breeze from Calvary's Hill*, and he asked them to sing it tenderly, and as they instantly and beautifully responded, everybody knew the prayer was answered.

He began to talk about that verse, "For such the Father seeks," but he soon got to the theme of self-sacrifice, as suggested and required by the great love of which they had been singing. "Do you say the call for self-sacrifice is hard? Not harder than for the Son to leave the Father's house. Is it dark? Not darker than Calvary."

The transition from this to *When I Survey the Wondrous Cross*, was most apt and impressive, and the feeling was almost too intense to be endured. For an hour nearly everything had been in Welsh, and then the English were so stirred that first one and then another prayed and testified, and for the next hour it was nearly all English. Evan Roberts himself shed tears of gratitude and was moved to speak briefly in English, and told how he was receiving letters from

England, Scotland, Ireland, Norway, France, Spain, America, and Africa.

After this the Welsh tongue prevailed, and one minister from North Wales thanked God that Snowdon was being shaken by the prayers of the quarrymen. And whilst nine or ten people were praying at the same time, without any semblance of disorder, the congregation sang very gently and softly in a faint undertone, in which the four parts were beautifully blended, *Oh, Send the Holy Spirit, Lord.*

The effect of this soft musical accompaniment to the prayers of several voices cannot be described. It is deeply impressive, and often leads the soul into a quiet ecstasy that is truly of Heaven. I believe it would be impossible for us to imitate this special feature of the revival worthily in England. I know one instance where it was attempted, and it was a ghastly failure, culminating only in a horrible medley of discordant noises suggestive of pandemonium, or worse. And there are one or two other features in which the Welsh excel, which we may well admire, but not imitate. We shall just prove ourselves ungainly and awkward in attempting to do what we cannot.

The evening meeting was at the other end of the village, at the Tabernacle. Here, too, there were about 1,500 people crammed into a chapel that would look very full with 900. The windows in the lobby were taken out to prevent suffocation, and the doors were wide open, but whilst this arrangement let in air, for which we were thankful, it also admitted sounds, for which we were not. Although a large overflow meeting was held at Horeb Baptist Chapel there was still a surging crowd in the street, and the police said there were thousands. This is very like an exaggeration, and yet there were probably more outside than there were in. The huge throng distressed and alarmed the babies and their mothers, and they all disturbed us, except when we were singing, and such glorious harmony nothing could disturb. It soothed the disappointed hosts outside, and as soon as we stopped Babel began again.

Ordinarily this would have been fatal to a really good meeting, and it was a very serious hindrance, but it was astonishing with what tact and patience and judgment Evan Roberts led us on step by step to disregard these distractions, till in the last half hour we gained a glorious victory, and finished the day with hallelujahs.

I found myself next to Rev. Llewellyn Morgan, of Neath Abbey, in the Swansea (Welsh) Circuit. The membership of his church was 142, and the revival has brought him seventy more, including several who had given up attendance at any place of worship. This is proportionately one of the largest increases recorded among our Wesleyan churches. One young man who prayed fervently was the organist of our little chapel at Pontardawe, and another lad of sixteen from the same place also prayed with wonderful force and passion. Both of these have only learned to pray in the revival.

One old man asked God to melt all the icebergs in the churches, and this led a London vicar to thank God that "the symbol of Christianity is not ice (although to judge by some Christians we should think it was), but fire—not wild fire, but holy fire." The next brother did not seem to be so afraid of wild fire, for he asked God that we might "get on fire with such big flames that no one could put them out."

In England everybody knows that grand old song, *The Lost Chord.* In Wales recently at their singing festivals one of their best-known songs has been a lamentation over "The Lost Amen." But in the revival the lost has been found, and nothing has been more surely recovered than the Amen. So now a stirring melody has been composed rejoicing in the *Return of the Amen.* At this evening's service a peasant girl with eyes shut, and as if completely absorbed in her theme, declaimed this new song with magnificent effect, and it succeeded in rousing to the full that national fervor that is so inimitable. It was a wonderful effort, and there wasn't a Welsh heart that wasn't stirred or a Welsh face that wasn't wet with tears.

Later on in this service Evan Roberts put a searching question which he has put once before, but not when I have been present, "Will those of you who have done your best for Jesus stand up?" Six or eight near me in the big pew, including two London clergymen well known at the Keswick meetings, immediately arose, but no one else in that crowded assembly seemed prepared to bear such a testimony. Personally I dared not, for this reason: I honestly believed I had done my best for Him as far as quantity was concerned, but when I thought of the quality of this quantity, it was far from satisfactory to me, and so I was sure its defects would be still more glaring in God's white light. And so I sat still and asked instead, as a devout woman did last week, "Lord, make me like a white sheet of paper without blots."

As the meeting came to a close about ten o'clock I witnessed a scene the like of which I have not known before. Evan Roberts called upon Christian people to stand and testify in the words of Scripture. First people rose in dozens, then in scores, next in hundreds, and all of them quietly and reverently quoting Scripture. No one shouted. It was a most exhilarating exercise, and as the faces of the witnesses beamed with the joy of the Lord I could only ascribe the glory to Him who hath "washed us from our sins in His own blood, and made us kings and priests unto God."

Delightful tidings reach us of the success of Mr. George Clark at Newport, Mr. Herbert Booth at Cardiff, and Gipsy Smith at Pontypridd. But the finest work of all is being done by a glorious company of enthusiastic and aggressive churches in almost every town and village in South Wales. These churches receive no extraneous aid, but they are depending solely on the power and presence of the Holy Spirit manifested in answer to importunate prayer and self-denying activity, and there are being added to these churches daily those that are being saved. Wales is resounding with doxologies. The mountains and the hills have broken into singing, and in our generation we have never before heard the like. One of the finest laymen Methodism has in the far North said to me on Tuesday, "I have been praying for this for years, and I was beginning to fear I should have to die without the sight; but it has come at last, and now won't I praise Him!"

London Methodist Times

REPORT BY WILLIAM T. STEAD

WILLIAM T. STEAD

Among those who have gone to see for themselves what is going on in Wales, is Mr. Wm. T. Stead, the famous London editor, a man of quick insight and about as little likely to mistake mere excitement or fanaticism for spiritual power as any one could well be.

The *London Methodist Times* says that this was Mr. Stead's first visit to the scene of a religious revival, and one of its representatives interviewed him about it on his return. Here is the interview:

"Well. Mr. Stead, you've been to the revival. What do you think of it?"

"Sir," said Mr. Stead, "the question is not what I think of it, but what it thinks of me, of you, and all the rest of us. For it is a very real thing, this revival, a live thing which seems to have a power and a grip which may get hold of a good many of us who at present are mere spectators."

"Do you think it is on the march, then?"

"A revival is something like a revolution. It is apt to be wonderfully catching. But you can never say. Look at the way the revolutionary tempest swept over Europe in 1848. But since then revolutions have not spread much beyond the border of the state in which they break out. We may have become immune to revivals, gospel hardened, or totally indifferent. I don't think so. But I would not like to prophesy."

"But in South Wales the revival is moving?"

"It reminded me," said Mr. Stead, "of the effect which travelers say is produced on the desert by the winds which propel the sandstorms, beneath which whole caravans have been engulfed. The wind springs up, no one knows from whence. Its eddying gusts lick up the sands, and soon the whole desert is filled with moving columns of sand, swaying and dancing and whirling as if they were instinct (filled. Ed.) with life. Woe be to the unprotected traveler whose path the sandstorm traverses."

"Then do you feel that we are in the track of the storm?"

"Can our people sing? That is the question to be answered before you can decide that. Hitherto the revival has not strayed beyond the track of the singing people. It has followed the line of song, not of preaching. It has sung its way from one end of South Wales to the other. But then the Welsh are a nation of singing birds."

"You speak as if you dreaded the revival coming your way."

"No, that is not so. Dread is not the right word. Awe expresses my sentiment better. For you are in the presence of the unknown. I tell you it is a live thing this revival, and if it gets hold of the people in London, for instance, it will make a pretty considerable shaking up."

"But surely it will be all to the good?"

"Yes, for the good, or for those who are all good. But what about those who are not good, or who, like the most of us, are a pretty mixed lot? Henry Ward Beecher used to say that if God were to answer the Lord's Prayer, and cause His will to be done in earth as it is in heaven, there were streets in New York which would be wrecked as if they had been struck by a tornado. Of course, it may be all to the good that we should be all shaken up; and tornadoes clear the air, and earthquakes are wholesome, but they are not particularly welcome to those who are at ease in Zion."

"Sandstorms of the desert, tornadoes, earthquakes: really, Mr. Stead, your metaphors would imply that your experiences in South Wales have been pretty bad?"

"No," said Mr. Stead. "Not bad at all. Do you remember what the little Quaker child said, when the Scottish express rushed at full speed through the station on the platform on which he was standing? 'Were you not frightened, my boy?' said his father. 'Oh, no,' said the little chap, 'a feeling of sweet peace stole into my mind.' I felt like that, rather. But the thing is awesome. You don't believe in ghosts?"

"Not much. I'll believe them when I see one."

"Well, you have read ghost stories, and can imagine what you would feel if you were alone at midnight in the haunted chamber of some old castle, and you heard the slow and stealthy step stealing along the corridor where the visitant from the other world was said to walk. If you go to South Wales and watch the revival you will feel pretty much like that. There is something there from the other world. You cannot say whence it came or whither it is going, but it moves and lives and reaches for you all the time. You see men and women go down in sobbing agony before your eyes as the invisible Hand clutches at their heart. And you shudder. It's pretty grim, I tell you. If you are afraid of strong emotions, you'd better give the revival a wide berth."

"But is it all emotion? Is there no teaching?"

"Precious little. Do you think that teaching is what people want in a revival? These people, all the people in a land like ours, are taught to death, preached to insensibility. They all know the essential truths. They know that they are not living as they ought to live, and no amount of teaching will add anything to that conviction.

"To hear some people talk you would imagine that the best way to get a sluggard out of bed is to send a tract on astronomy showing him that according to the fixed and eternal law the sun will rise at a certain hour in the morning. The sluggard does not deny it. He is entirely convinced of it. But what he knows is that it is precious cold at sunrise on a winter's morning, and it is very snug and warm between the blankets. What the sluggard needs is to be well shaken, and in case of need to be pulled out of bed. 'Roused,' the revival calls it. And the revival is a rouser rather than a teacher.

"And that is why I think those churches which want to go on dozing in the ancient ways had better hold a special series of prayer meetings that the revival may be prevented coming their way."

"Then I take it that your net impressions were favorable?"

"How could they be otherwise? Did I not feel the pull of that unseen Hand? And have I not heard the glad outburst of melody that hailed the confession of some who in very truth had found salvation? Of course it is all very much like what I have seen in the Salvation Army. I was delighted to see that at last the Welsh churches are recognizing the equal ministry of men and women. The surging waters are right on the very beach of the movement. There is a wonderful spontaneity about it all, and so far its fruits have been good and only good."

"Will it last?"

"Nothing lasts forever in this mutable world. And the revival will no more last than the blossom lasted in the field in springtime. But if the blossom had not come and gone, there would be no bread in the world today. And as it is with the bread which Mr. Chamberlain would tax, so it is with that other bread which is the harvest that will be gathered in long after this revival has taken its place in history. But if the analogy of all previous revivals holds good, this religious awakening will be influencing for good the lives of numberless men and women who will be living and toiling and carrying on the work of this God's world of ours, long after you and I have been gathered to our fathers."

THIRTY-FOUR THOUSAND CONVERSIONS IN WALES

BY GEORGE T. B DAVIS

I have just returned from a two days' visit to the storm center of the great Welsh revival which is sweeping over Wales like a cyclone, lifting people into an ecstasy of spiritual fervor. Already over 34,000 converts have been made, and the great awakening shows no signs of waning. All observers agree that the movement is fully as remarkable as the memorable revival of 1859-60. It is sweeping over hundreds of hamlets and cities, emptying saloons, theaters, and dance halls, and filling the churches night after night with praying multitudes. The policemen are almost idle; in many cases the magistrates have few trials on hand; debts are being paid; and the character of entire communities is being transformed almost in a day. Wales is studded with coal mines, and it is a common occurrence to have prayer meetings held a thousand feet under ground amid the tinkle of the horses' bells and the weird twinkle of the miners' lamps.

Mr. Lloyd George, a member of Parliament, and the foremost Welsh statesman of the day, speaks of the awakening as a great earthquake. He says, "All those who love Wales must wish the revival Godspeed. It is certainly the most remarkable spiritual movement this generation has witnessed. Personally I believe it is destined to leave a permanent mark on the history of our country. The most important thing to urge in connection with it is that the religious leaders of Wales should see in time that the great forces which have been aroused into activity should not be wasted in mere outbursts of emotion. Let them in time overhaul their denominational machinery, and adapt it to the new and greater demand upon its resources which has been created by this remarkable upheaval, which seems to be rocking Welsh life like a great earthquake."

The leader of the revival is Mr. Evan Roberts, a young man only twenty-six years of age, who was a collier, and was later apprenticed to become a blacksmith. Then he felt a call to the ministry, and was a student in a preparatory school when the Spirit came upon him in such power that he felt impelled to return to his native village of Loughor and tell the people of God's love for them. He did so, and, as he spoke the fire fell from heaven upon the community. The people were so inflamed that they crowded church after church until four o'clock in the morning. The flame spread from district to district throughout South Wales with almost incredible swiftness, and soon scores of towns were being shaken by the power of God. From the beginning, however, Mr. Roberts has been the leader of the movement, and wherever he goes the revival reaches fever heat. The foremost Welsh newspapers devote columns to his meetings daily, and his photographs and souvenir postcards representing him are sold everywhere. Some idea of his sudden fame may be gained from the fact that sixty newspaper representatives endeavored to interview him in two days recently.

It was my good fortune to take two meals with Mr. Roberts, and to attend three meetings he conducted. But let me give the readers of the *Witness* my impressions of the meetings and of Mr. Roberts in order as they were formed during the visit.

At noon on Tuesday I wired one of the leading Welsh newspapers, asking where Mr. Roberts would speak that evening. The reply came back that he would be at Swansea for the next two days. At 2 P. M. I left Liverpool with an American friend, and we arrived at Swansea at 9:30 P. M. Hastening to a hotel we found it filled with visitors, who had come to "catch the fire" of the revival. A second place we found in a similar condition, but at the third place we secured accommodation, and then hastened to the church, which was fortunately situated in the downtown district. It was 9:45 when we reached the place, and even at that hour there were some scores of people in the street seeking admission. But the gates were closed and guarded by policemen, for the church was already packed to the doors. Going up to one of the policemen I whispered that I was an American journalist, and that my friend and I were from Chicago. These words acted like a magic charm, for he at once asked us to come to another gate, where we were speedily admitted and ushered into the building. My first impression! How am I to describe it? As we entered the door I beheld a room, meant to seat about 700 people, crowded to suffocation with about 1,500. But this was not the chief thing that attracted us. Up in the gallery a young lady—almost a girl—was standing, praying with such a fervor as I had rarely, if ever, witnessed before. One hand was upraised, and her tones were full of agonized pleading, and though it was in Welsh, so that I could not understand a word she uttered, yet it sent a strange thrill through me. Then a young man arose, and with rapt upraised face prayed as though he were in the presence of the

Almighty. The entire atmosphere of the room was white-hot with spiritual emotion, and my chief thought was, "This is a picture of what must have occurred in the early church in the first century of the Christian era."

A hymn was now started, and my attention was riveted on Evan Roberts, who stood in the pulpit and led the music with face irradiated with joy, smiles, and even laughter. What impressed me most was his utter naturalness, his entire absence of solemnity. He seemed just bubbling over with sheer happiness, just as jubilant as a young man at a baseball game. He did not preach; he simply talked between the prayers and songs and testimonies, and then rarely more than a few sentences at a time. Imagine a Christian Endeavor meeting where those present are wrought up to a pitch of holy enthusiasm until they are literally "on fire," and you will have an accurate picture of the proceedings at Trinity Chapel that night.

To my surprise the meeting terminated at 10:30. The reason for this, it was explained, is that Swansea is a city of nearly 100,000 population, and the people must go to their work early the next morning; and also that Mr. Roberts was usually ending the meetings at about this hour so as to avoid a nervous collapse.

The next morning my friend and I went to the place where Mr. Roberts was staying, and were not only successful in securing a cordial interview, but were also invited to have luncheon with him. In appearance the young evangelist is of medium height, slender, brown-haired. He is extremely nervous in temperament, and his pallor showed the strain of the meetings upon him. When asked for a message for America, he grasped my hand, and gave me the following, "The prophecy of Joel is being fulfilled. There the Lord says, 'I will pour out My Spirit upon all flesh.' If that is so, all flesh must be prepared to receive. (1) The past must be clear; every sin confessed to God, any wrong to man must be put right. (2) Everything doubtful must be removed once for all out of our lives. (3) Obedience prompt and implicit to the Spirit of God. (4) Public confession of Christ. Christ said, 'I, if I be lifted up will draw all men unto Me.' There it is. Christ is all in all."

The afternoon and evening meetings we attended were very largely like the first one, save that in each meeting the mood of Mr. Roberts was different. At the afternoon meeting, while describing the agony of Christ in the Garden of Gethsemane, he broke down and sobbed from the pulpit, while scores in the building wept with him. The meeting had been announced to begin at 2 P. M., but before 12 the building was packed, although it was at the edge of the city. It was with the utmost difficulty, aided by the police, that your correspondent and his friend squeezed themselves in at the rear door, and then we stood near the pulpit scarcely able to move an arm. The air was stifling, but the people minded this not a whit. They had forgotten the things of earth, and stood in the presence of God. The meeting began about noon, and went on at white heat for two hours before Mr. Roberts arrived, ending at 4:30 P. M.

At the evening meeting Mr. Roberts was silent much of the time. For full twenty minutes he sat or stood motionless with closed eyes. But the meeting went on just as fervidly as though he were speaking.

It was strange indeed to hear some one praying undisturbed while a hymn was being sung; or to hear two, three, or four engaged in prayer at the same time; yet, as has been so often remarked, there was perfect order in the midst of the seeming disorder. It was the Lord's doing, and it was marvelous in our eyes! Presently a young girl—not over sixteen years of age—arose in the gallery, and began to pray. I understood not a word she said, but in a few seconds, in spite of myself, the tears were streaming down my cheeks. I looked up, and lo! Old gray-haired ministers of the gospel were likewise weeping! There was a something in the very tones of her voice that lifted one above the world, and pierced to the core of one's heart. I learned later that she was pleading with God that certain people might be reconciled with her. She loved them, but they did not love her, and she pleaded that they might be led to do so that night.

It was nearly 10 P. M. when the most thrilling and beautiful incident of our visit occurred. A respectably dressed young man of about nineteen came down from the gallery, crying like a child, the tears streaming down his face as he tottered through the aisle towards the "set fawr" (This was sometimes a bench-like seat where the deacons sat. Could also be the "big seat" at the front of a chapel, slightly elevated and facing the pulpit. Ed.). He was nearly fainting when he got to the entrance to the big seat, and he threw his arms around the neck of the Rev. William James, the pastor of Ebenezer, which is the church he attends.

"Pray for me! Pray for me!" he shouted, as he embraced the minister, who was moved to tears. The young man dropped into a chair. Mr. Roberts, who had been sitting on a chair in the pulpit, was on his feet. Something seemed to have told him what was the matter, and his face beamed with joy. Down the pulpit stairs he proceeded, and, on reaching the young man, threw his arms around him in a most affectionate manner. Mr. Roberts talked to him, and in a few minutes both were on their way to the pulpit. The young man was in first. What a change! The symptoms of being overcome had disappeared. His face had never worn a brighter appearance! "Is mother here? Is mother here?" he shouted. A voice from the back of the chapel answered, "Yes! Yes! She's here!"

At this point every one in the audience was so deeply touched by the affecting scene that there was scarcely a dry eye to be observed. Some one started the Welsh hymn which is always sung when a person yields completely to God, and which has become the chant of victory of the revival. In thrilling and triumphant tones they sang fervently:

"Diolch iddo, diolch iddo, diolch iddo,
Byth am golio, llwch as llawr."
Which being interpreted means :
"Praises, praises, praises to God
Who has remembered such as we are."

When all was quiet, he said, "Mother, I have had to give in! Yes, indeed! I tried to refuse, but I was compelled to submit!"

A little later on he was calling for others to surrender, as it was "grand." He would not give his mother any more trouble! The mother broke into prayer, and when her son recognized her voice, he shouted, "Well done, mam!" (Well done, mother).

It is little wonder that Gipsy Smith, a prominent English evangelist, after spending a Sunday in the midst of the revival witnessing the remarkable scenes, said, "My visit to Wales last Sunday deepens my conviction that the movement now passing over Wales is a great and blessed Scriptural revival, and ought not to be called 'The Welsh Revival,' but 'The Religious Revival,' for I believe it will shake England, and why not the world? This is the Acts of the Apostles up-to-date."

Numerous accounts have been given of the beginning of the mighty awakening, no two of which agree. Some attribute it to a young girl who spoke at a Christian Endeavor meeting with such fervor that her hearers were melted into tears, and the flame started there. Others declare that it began when Evan Roberts went back to his native town of Loughor, two months ago, and set it on fire with his Spirit-filled pleading to accept Christ. But the fact is that the revival broke out in a score of places almost simultaneously, and Evan Roberts and the other young and fiery evangelists who have arisen during the last few weeks are largely the products rather than the causes of the awakening.

The true origin of the movement is probably to be found in the prayer circles which have honeycombed Wales for the last eighteen months. The people who had banded themselves together were crying out mightily for a revival, and God at length graciously answered the prayers of His saints. And it is interesting to Americans to know how the prayer circles were started. A lady living in Australia read a book by Dr. Torrey in which he reiterated the statement that we must "pray through." At that time Dr. Torrey and Mr. Alexander were conducting their great revival in Melbourne, the success of which was largely due to the 2,000 prayer circles which existed throughout the city. Shortly afterward the lady came to England and was the means of starting thousands of prayer circles throughout the United Kingdom, the object of which was to pray for a worldwide revival. The answer has come in part in the Welsh awakening, and may God speed the day when the fire will spread over all the United Kingdom, and over America, and throughout the entire world!

New York Weekly Witness

DRUNKENNESS AND BLASPHEMY DISAPPEAR

Reports from all the districts in South Wales affected by the revival show that the Christmas holidays, so dreaded by new converts who formerly devoted the whole of the time to drink and revelry, have passed by without the defections from the faith loudly prophesied by the unsympathetic and unbelieving. South Wales has never known such a quiet and peaceful Christmas.

In Cardiff alone, as yet only slightly moved by the revival, police reports show that drunkenness has diminished 60 per cent, whilst on Saturday last the Mayor was presented by the chief constable with a pair of white gloves, there being no case at all on the charge sheet—an unprecedented fact for the last day of the year.

The same thing happened at the Swansea County Court on the previous Saturday, and the magistrate said, "All the years I've been sitting here

I've never seen anything like it, and I attribute this happy state of things entirely to the revival."

The streets of Aberdare on Christmas Eve were almost entirely free from drunkenness, and on Christmas Day there were no prisoners at all in the cells.

At Pontypridd, *mirablie dictu* (wonderful to relate. Ed.), there were no assaults on the police, and throughout the mining area generally drunkenness was the exception and not the rule.

At Abercarn Police Court, responsible for a population of 21,000, there was not a single summons on Thursday—a thing unknown since the court was formed fourteen years ago—and here, too, was enacted the ceremony of the white gloves.

Bridgend Station, usually the scene of much debauchery on the part of drunken excursionists going to and from Cardiff, has never known such orderly behavior, and the streets of the town, too, have been free from rowdyism. Similar reports come from Carmarthen and other important centers, such as Merthyr.

Many of the miners in Glamorganshire come from small towns and villages in North Wales, and the trains conveying them to their old homes for Christmas were jubilant with revival song. At Machynlleth, on the Cambrian, where the Aberystwith and Barmouth portions of the train had to be divided, the passengers from both congregated on the platform and held a prayer meeting. Throughout the holiday season the chapels in most places were open for prayer and praise meetings morning, afternoon, and night, and to these places the people thronged with delight, and spent their time and their energies in strengthening the weak and rescuing the tempted. Railway returns show that the excursion holiday traffic has been reduced by one-half, the people evidently preferring to remain at home to pray and sing in company with those recently reclaimed.

There has been a correspondent reduction in public house takings (receipts. Ed.) and in attendances at low-class places of amusement. Third and fourth rate theatrical touring companies, who usually reap such a rich harvest in these regions at Christmas, have found it advisable to keep clear of the Rhondda this time.

Restitution still holds a prominent place in the revival program. One conscience-stricken traveler hands over 1S. 7d. (British shilling & pence. Ed.) to the Rhymney Railway Company, in payment of a nineteen miles journey some time ago without a ticket. A Rhymney business firm acknowledges the receipt of £5 (British pounds. Ed.) from an anonymous person in payment of an old debt, long disregarded. A collier, who has formerly spent his money on all kinds of sinful pleasure, has removed his younger brother from an orphanage, and has decided to support him with his savings till he is old enough to provide for himself.

At one service a man with a tear-stained face rushed from the gallery to a pew downstairs, and, clutching passionately the hand of another man, entreated to be forgiven. It was evidently a request not easily granted, so the two repaired to the vestry, where the wrong was satisfactorily rectified, and then the two men newly-reconciled returned to take a happier part in the service.

The conscience of the community, as well as of the church, seems to be quickened. At Pontypridd for years past it has been customary to give bottles of whisky as prizes in connection with the volunteer shooting competition; but this year every man who formerly gave a drink prize has given a money prize instead.

The change in the language of the crowds has been just as marked this Christmas as the change in their drinking habits. This change cannot be more suitably expressed than in the two verses which have now disappeared from that well-known hymn, No. 366, in our new book:

> Suffice that for the season past
> Hell's horrid language filled our tongues,
> We all Thy words behind us east,
> And lewdly sang the drunkard's songs.
>
> But, O the power of grace divine!
> In hymns we now our voices raise,
> Loudly in strange hosannas join,
> And blasphemies are turned to praise!

Whilst bands of enthusiastic workers have paraded the streets, arresting the attention of the careless by joyful song and earnest invitation, homely meetings have been extemporized in cottages, and here some of the most precious experiences of the revival have been obtained. "The church in the house" is very precious in the sight of the Father. At one of these family gatherings no less than five conversions were recorded on the evening of Boxing

Day. For such it was a happy prelude to the Crowning Day, which all true believers anticipate.

The secular press is still fanning the flame by its sympathetic reports of the revival meetings. Surely the most remarkable fact yet recorded in daily journalism is the "Revival Edition" of the *Evening Express,* published in Cardiff on the *27th* ult (of the last month. Ed.) The managers have found a football edition to pay them well, so they experimented on Tuesday week with a "Revival Edition," in which every article, every report, every paragraph, and every portrait, indeed every line, except the advertisements, dealt with religious work. It has had such an enormous sale that a similar edition was produced this last Tuesday.

The Bishops of Bangor and St. David's have both guardedly blessed the revival in their pastorals, but the finest tribute comes from the saintly and Evangelical Bishop of Durham, who appeals to his brethren in the ministry everywhere "to observe this movement with a reverent welcome and sacred hope."

The young missionaries have given themselves a very little rest. Evan Roberts attended the evening service at Moriah Chapel, Longhor, on the evening of Christmas Day. He listened to a sermon on immortality from the resident minister, and then conducted a vigorous and inspiring after meeting, and did not leave the chapel till 10:30 P. M. This has long been the chapel of his ancestors. His great-grandfather, a fine soldier, who was wounded at Waterloo, worshiped here, and was honored for his sterling piety. His grandfather, who, as his father does now, worked at the adjoining colliery, was also a prominent worshiper here and an ardent missioner (evangelist, crusader. Ed.) in the temperance cause in the days of its unpopularity; and it was in this very chapel that this young miner student, fresh from his

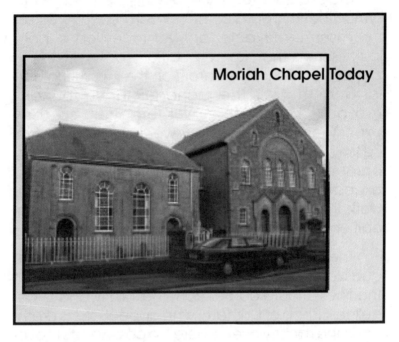

Moriah Chapel Today

studies at the Newcastle Emlyn Grammar School, conducted those inspiring services less than three months ago which immediately preceded the outburst, or downpour, with which everybody is now familiar. Dr. Cynddylan Jones, that great preacher to preachers, says of this, "To work up a revival is to try to save the world by mechanics. The Heaven-sent man draws down a revival, saves men by dynamics. The gospel of mechanics is a cumbrous, costly machine, the gospel of dynamics—power from on high, without machinery and guarantees—goes straight to the heart, and accomplishes that for which it is sent. I am not ashamed of the gospel of Christ, for it is the dynamic of God unto salvation. And today the dynamic is working. Is it a marvel that there are explosions? And where there are explosions is it a marvel that there is confusion? Out of the chaos will emerge the kosmos; out of confusion, order and beauty and life."

Though preaching is not generally acceptable at these spontaneous meetings, for *enthusiastic song and fervent prayer* and heart-stirring confession hold the field, yet the reading of God's Word is always welcome, and in the most lively meetings I have attended I have not known a deeper interest manifested in anything than in the reading of the Scriptures. Every verse is punctuated with heartfelt responses, and the poorest reader is thus encouraged by such prayerful sympathy to give the testimony of the Word side by side with the testimony of man.

At Clydach, in the Swansea Valley, where Evan Roberts began his second campaign on the 28th ult (in the preceding month, Ed.), there were the same unwieldy crowds and the same jubilant song that he meets with everywhere. He seems to get less and less patient with the ravenous curiosity to see the mere man. He is in no sense flattered by it, and his heart grieves over it more and more. "It kills me to see people paying me too much attention. Grace must conquer that." Again and again I have seen him wrestle in the pulpit in tearful and agonizing prayer, till he and the congregation have got the victory over that unspiritual besetment of curiosity that takes mind and heart off the real business in hand, and prevents people from seeing Jesus only.

From Clydach Evan Roberts moved to Morriston, where the revival had secured a great hold upon the population. This is vouched for by the fact that in the preceding week the churches had reaped from 1,300 to 1,400 converts. No wonder then that 2,500 people crowded into the large chapel to hear him and that other chapels were also filled. On Sunday he had three services at Pentre-Estyll, on the outskirts of Swansea. Here, too, for weeks past the churches had been all aflame, and Sunday's services were profoundly impressive. One man, fearful of the harm done by man worship, said of Evan Roberts in prayer, "Lord, put him out of sight," but another prayed, "Use him as a speaking trumpet." Some of the young evangelist's saying here were expressive and forcible.

Speaking of emotionalism, he said: "If there is to be no feeling in this world, I am afraid you will have too much of it in the next."

"Some men try to get one arm around the world and the other 'round heaven—they want both."

"I am afraid some people's heaven will be a very small one. They want to go to heaven on tip-toes, without anybody knowing it. I fear nobody will know they are there."

Elsewhere other young evangelists are at work, and the movement gathers force day by day. The services at the Welsh Tabernacle at Cardiff continue to be very effective in reclaiming some of the most abandoned. Principal Edwards says they are "at close grips with the evil one," and some of the services have been disturbed by young atheists. Again and again serious consequences have been averted by the tactful and pathetic (passionate. Ed.) singing of Miss A. M. Rees.

There is also a hard struggle going on in Newport, but it cannot as yet be said that there is any great development there. But as time goes on hopefulness abounds more and more, and every one knows there is good reason for it.

London Methodist Time
January 5

Influence on the Severn Valley Mission
Sixty-six New Members on Trial

There are various and unmistakable signs of the revival in this mission. In one town, under the ministry of the resident minister, a new spirit has come over the church, which can be traced in every department; prayer meetings are largely attended, class meetings are alive and are remarkably powerful and blessed, open-air services are held with manifestations of divine awe and influence. A few items in detail may be of interest. The annual tea party in one place usually accompanied by innocent games had to be turned into a prayer and testimony meeting when souls were quickened and converted. An open-air meeting was held in one of the marketplaces preparatory to an indoor service, but such a wave of power came upon the crowd of some three hundred people that for two hours the meeting continued, believers singing solos, bearing their testimony, and praying in the Holy Ghost, some of whom have been silent and timid in the past. One class leader tells how the room was full of persons, but better still, the persons were filled with a divine enthusiasm, and it was impossible to close the meeting until after eleven o'clock.

A wonderful story, might be told of what has occurred in another town, especially if all the details were given. It started with the conversion of one of the students of a Welsh university at the ordinary Sunday evening service conducted by the Superintendent of the Mission. Recently this student with five others who have been saved visited the united prayer meetings held in the town, and among other strange things that have happened in connection with these students has been the conversion of the Calvinistic minister. He has made a public confession which has caused quite a sensation among the religious community, to say nothing of the inhabitants of the town. He tells how he left one of the meetings determined to burn all his sermons, and how the devil tempted him to save two for Sunday, but amid shouts of praise he told how he got the victory, and burnt the lot. The Holy Ghost has so filled his soul that he is preaching, praying, working, and living in a new world of light, liberty, and power.

The effects are widespread; enemies are becoming friends. Opposition and bitter feelings in church services have ceased. Unity, harmony, are working miracles. Over one hundred persons have already publicly confessed Christ at one of our chapels, and "the number of believers is being multiplied." Everybody sings now in wonderful power with heart and voice, the more verses the better. It is thrilling to hear them singing *There shall be Showers of Blessing*, in the open air and indoors, with or without the musical instrument; *Hail, Thou once Despised Jesus*, to the tune *Hyfrydol*; *Jesus, Lover of My Soul*, to *Aberystwyth*; *For You I am Praying*, and *The Glory Song*.

The old Methodist hymns are quite new in this gracious spirit of revival, and God is blessing them to crowds.

On Thursday the Quarterly Meeting of the Mission was held in the Lecture Hall, which was full. The local preachers were delighted to authorize the formation of two more Mission Bands to help to evangelize the villages, and one excellent young man was received "on trial." One of the ministers gave an earnest appeal to the brethren to seek the burden of souls and strive to bring persons to immediate decision for Christ in their services. The great official meeting was held in the afternoon, and the opening hymn was sung with real Welsh revival spirit, and the praying was mighty, and unitedly joined in. The business was entered into with a beautiful spirit, and various forward movements were adopted. A commission was appointed to investigate the affairs of the small places in one of the sections of the Mission, and a committee appointed to arrange a United Musical Festival for the purpose of helping congregational singing and stimulating the various choirs. A very gratifying numerical statement was presented showing another increase in membership, with no less than one hundred and four "on trial," being sixty-six added during the quarter. The finances showed a much healthier state, with brighter prospects for the future. The doxology was sung most unitedly and heartily. After an enjoyable tea a capital open-air demonstration was held under the big lamp in the town, and was carried on half-an-hour after time, but no one complained. The power of God was with us, and the attention of the crowd of working people was remarkable. The best-attended public meeting we have seen here was held in the chapel.

It was easy to speak, pray, and sing, and the power of the Lord was present to heal.

Methodist Times

The Welsh Revival

The Vicar of Burley, Leeds, has evidently made up his mind about the value of this movement, judging by his advertisement in *The South Wales Daily News.*

"WELSH REVIVAL— Curate wanted . . . Warm welcome for bright, earnest, fiery, genial Welshman . . ."

There are plenty of that type in evidence just now, and their number is rapidly increasing, though only a very small proportion are in holy orders. The joyousness of this revival is more and more manifest as the weeks go by. The first week of the year has given it a yet mightier impetus, and it has a wider sweep than ever. There is no abatement, and no sign of it. Everybody recognizes that the tide is flowing faster, and churches that till quite recently were stuck fast on the mud banks and looked forbidding and unlovely, are now being cleansed and refreshed and beautified by the living waters. The large towns, with their larger English element, are now receiving the baptism that at first was bestowed almost exclusively upon the Welsh community in the mining districts. The visit of Evan Roberts to Swansea has been a great blessing to him and to all associated with him, and it has very perceptibly quickened the evangelistic fervor of all the churches. And when we say "all" we mean all. For in Swansea, following the example of the Vicar, the Hon. Talbot Rice, everybody who is anybody in the religious life of that locality was present at Ebenezer, where the late Dr. Rees, the historian of Welsh Congregationalism once ministered. It was indeed a thrilling scene. There in the pulpit stood the youthful evangelist, a native of a neighboring mining village. Three months ago he was unheard of and unknown, and now around him are clustered the representative leaders of all sections of the church of Christ, sympathetically and enthusiastically following his lead because he is led of the Spirit. It is a happy augury (omen, prophecy. Ed.). God's man is the man of the future, and the men of God are assured of victory when God's purpose becomes their own and they make this their motto. "This one thing I do."

The chapel was filling rapidly at eleven. This means that when Evan Roberts arrived a very large proportion had been there for nearly four hours. Indeed, before one o'clock the gates leading to the chapel were *locked and guarded by the police*, and a crowd of many hundreds in the streets were being directed to the overflow meetings.

Those who have seen most of the meetings elsewhere declare that this appeared to be the most joyous and jubilant of them all. As he entered, the people were singing with much *hwyl* (passion and fervor. Ed.):

> "Rhy fyr yw tragwyddoleb llawn
> I ddyweyd yn iawn am dano.
> (Too short is all eternity to tell the Savior's story)."

"Do you believe it, *my* friends?" he asked. He then proceeded to dwell on God's greatest gift. "What do we give in return? The collection plate comes around, and we dip into our pockets and bring forth—a copper. God's greatest, man's least. God couldn't give more; man couldn't give less. Let men keep their scraps. Give God all. You cannot compete with God in giving. Just try. The more *you* give, the more God will give in return."

Sweetly led by Miss Annie Davies, the huge congregation rose and sang with overwhelming power and pathos a hymn of full surrender, which brought everybody to the very gate of heaven.

ANNIE DAVIES

Then a young woman from Llanelly, with charming simplicity and choking voice, told how for long God's face had been hidden from her, and she felt she was cut adrift, till it pleased God to chasten her on a bed of suffering, and there she had a vision of Christ in His kingly robes; she "saw the King in His beauty," and that had set all right. She had been much persecuted for her religion, but her faith in Jesus was exultant. The effect of this inspiring testimony was tremendous. Let no one sneer at the part that woman is taking in this revival. God is greatly honoring her, and she is confessing Him by singing, praying, and testifying. A woman's voice is often heard when the woman herself cannot be seen. It is quite exceptional for there to be any obtruding of personality. What she does is generally done modestly, under the pressure of intense feeling and with a simplicity that reaches all hearts. Later on in the meeting a young man sprang to his feet and said under great excitement, "I have given myself to Christ. I have £11 in the bank; I will give that too." And here again Evan Roberts's common sense was as evident as his grace. "Amen. Give it to Him by all means, but keep the money until you are given an unmistakable indication what God would have you do with it."

Joyous surrender was the keynote of this service, and towards the close the young evangelist said, "There will soon be a great demand for funds, for missionaries will be plentiful. Hundreds have declined the call to proceed to the mission fields because they loved parents and friends more than they loved the Lord." Those who attended the first meetings of the revival in November and are able to compare Evan Roberts now with what he was then are greatly impressed with his growing power. One well qualified to judge says, "There is a wondrous change in him already. He has immensely improved. His voice has gained in sweetness and resonance, while he is never at a loss for a bright clear thought and plain, simple language in which to express it."

With so much liberty in these meetings it is astonishing that there is not more license. But here, too, the evangelist is learning by experience, and on two occasions this week he has stopped a few who ought to have been stopped long ago. "Stop! Stop! Some meetings have been spoiled so that other meetings may be saved. In this way I have learned wisdom, and so must you. You may quench the Spirit by wanting to show yourselves." In the same meeting at which this occurred a man said in Welsh, "Lord, we thank Thee for that extra turn of the screw we had just now." The next day at Llansamlet the curiosity to see the young evangelist was so keen that the first hour of the meeting—*was perceptibly chilled by it.*

He said, "One might think you have come here from the North Pole, but if you had passed Calvary you would be warmer than you are. This won't do. You are placing man before God. There are three spirits in this meeting—the Spirit of God, the spirit of man, and the evil spirit."

This brought Rev. Penar Griffiths up. He and his church have been abundantly blessed in this revival. "These meetings are too cheap," he declared. "Some of you say you have lost a day's work, have you lost a tear? Others of you say you have closed your shops, but have you opened your hearts?"

The thaw soon came, and then there followed a truly heart-searching incident. The evangelist invited those who had done their best for Christ to stand up. Many ministers and prominent church workers from far and near were present, and the chapel was thronged with eager Christians. For a minute or so all looked within, but no one dared to rise. At last a woman, whose eyes were red with weeping, stood and said, "I have tried to do my best for Him," and so said another. All through the audience it was evident the thought was prayerfully working, "Have I done my best?" and soon there came the confessions, voluntarily given, that have been so frank and stimulating in this revival. Said one minister, "I have felt since I remained seated that I have done my best for Jesus, but it has not been so clear and pure as it might have been." Then a very old man told how humbled he was, and how for two days prior to that meeting he had fasted prayerfully. Then a young working man rose and said how after yesterday's meeting he had been reconciled to a neighbor with whom he had been at variance for sixteen years. "He is here now," and pointed to the one concerned, who humbly acquiesced. Following these confessions there came uplifting song and mighty prayer, and a meeting that was icy to begin with was as consuming fire at the end.

The ethical results of this revival continue to be great and convincing. Everybody feels it is more than a coincidence that at the quarter sessions for the County of Glamorgan on Tuesday the judge was able to announce that the calendar was the lightest for twenty years, and that of the eleven cases only one was of a serious character.

Many people are devoting their energies to the establishment of rescue homes for the unfortunate victims of men's cruel lust, some of whom now are longing for deliverance and shelter.

The delegates of the Miners' Western District decided at Swansea to hold no more meetings in public houses. At the meeting of the Rhondda (No. 1) District of the Miners' Federation the chairman alluded to the revival, and hoped they would seek the guidance of the Spirit in commercial affairs, and so secure a more satisfactory settlement of their unfortunate disputes.

At Ystradgynlais, before a meeting of 1,500 people *three ministers who had publicly quarreled* about local politics and the administration of the Education Act, became publicly reconciled, and ended their animosities by cordially uniting in the soul-saving work of the revival. Similar results are of daily occurrence in commerce, in society, and in the church.

Cardiff is receiving a very gracious baptism, and our own churches are sharing blessedly in the results. There has been a distinct outpouring during the past week. At Roathroad, Broadway, and Splotroad there are constant conversions, and private advises from other Methodist centers show that our people are receiving and communicating the sacred fire.

The event of the week has been the publishing of the full and authentic account of Evan Roberts' experience as dictated by him on December 28 to Rev. T. Francis, Church Missionary minister, Gorseinon, by whom it has been translated into English. All Methodists will see in it a wonderful similarity to the narratives of God's dealings with the early Methodist preachers. The more important extracts will be deeply interesting to the readers of *The Methodist Times.*

London Times
January 12

EVAN ROBERTS' STORY

EVAN
ROBERTS
FROM A
POST
CARD.

"For thirteen years I had prayed for the Spirit, and this is the way I was led to pray. William Davies, the deacon, said one night in the society, 'Remember to be faithful. What if the Spirit descended and you absent? Remember Thomas! What a loss he had.' I said then to myself, 'I will have the Spirit.' And through all weather and in spite of all difficulties I went to the meetings. Many times on seeing other boys with the boats on the tide I was tempted to turn back and join them. But no. Then I said to myself, 'Remember your resolve to be faithful,' and on I went. Prayer meeting Monday evening at the chapel, prayer meeting Tuesday evening at Pisgah (Sunday school branch); church meeting, Wednesday; Band of Hope, Thursday; class, Friday evening—to these I went faithfully through the years. For ten or eleven years I have prayed for a revival. I could sit up all night to read or talk about revivals. It was the Spirit that moved me to think about this.

"One Friday night last spring, when praying by my bedside before retiring, I was taken up to a great expanse—without time and space. It was communion with God. Before this a far-off God I had. I was frightened that night, but never since. So great was my shivering that I rocked the bed, and my brother, being awakened, took hold of me, thinking I was ill.

"After that experience I was awakened every night a little after one o'clock. This was most strange, for through the years I slept like a rock, and no disturbance in my room would awaken me. From that hour I was taken up into the divine fellowship for about four hours. What it was I cannot tell you, except that it was divine. About five o'clock I was again allowed to sleep on till about nine.

"At this time I was again taken up into the same experience as in the earlier hours of the morning until about twelve or one o'clock . . . This went on for three months."

He then refers to the convention at Blaenaunerch, Cardiganshire, last August, "The seven o'clock meeting was devoted to asking and answering questions. Rev. W. W. Lewis conducted. At the close Rev. Seth Joshua prayed, and said during his prayer, 'Lord, do this, and this, and this, etc., and bend us.' He did not say, 'O Lord, bend us.' It was the Spirit that put the emphasis for me on 'Bend us.' 'That is what you need,' said the Spirit to me. And as I went out I prayed, 'O Lord, bend me.'

W. W. LEWIS

SETH JOSHUA

"On the way to the nine o'clock meeting Rev. Seth Joshua remarked, 'We are going to have a wonderful meeting today.' To this I replied, 'I feel myself almost bursting.'

"The meeting having been opened was handed over to the Spirit. I was conscious that I would have to pray. As one and the other prayed, I put the question to the Spirit, Shall I pray now?' 'Wait a while,' said He. When others prayed I felt a living force come into my bosom. I held my breath, and my legs shivered, and after every prayer I asked, 'Shall I now?' The living force grew and grew, and I was almost bursting. And instantly some one ended his prayer—my bosom boiling. I would have burst if I had not prayed. What boiled me was that verse, 'God commending His love.' I fell on my knees with my arms over the seat in front of me, and the tears and perspiration flowed freely. I thought blood was gushing forth.

"For about two minutes it was fearful. I cried, 'Bend me! Bend me! Bend us! . . .' What bent me was God commending His love (Rom. 5: 8), and I not seeing anything in it to commend. After I was bent a wave of peace came over me, and the audience sang, 'I hear thy welcome voice.' And as they sang I thought of the bending at the Judgment Day, and I was filled with compassion for those who would be bent on that day, and I wept.

"Henceforth the salvation of souls became the burden of my heart. From that time I was on fire with a desire to go through all Wales, and if it were possible I was willing to pay God to allow me to go. A plan was agreed upon, and eight of us were to go through Wales, and I was to pay all expenses."

In other parts of South Wales crowded and enthusiastic services are being held, and everywhere large numbers of inquirers are announced. At the Tabernacle in Cardiff a gang of gamblers has been broken up by the revival, and twelve of them have yielded to Christ. One of the Welsh hymns sung most fervently at all the services says:

"Gone is the morn, it's getting late,
But open still is mercy's gate."

And in at that gate hundreds are still flocking. A well-dressed shop assistant staggered to the front and asked a minister to pray for him. As soon as he found the Lord he got up and shouted out in Welsh, "Is mother here?" When he was told she was at the back of the chapel, he called out, "Mother, I've had to give in at last. I tried to refuse, but I was compelled."

And so the glorious work goes on.

GOD HATH VISITED HIS PEOPLE

God brings round His seasons in the spiritual world as in the natural, and there is none of them that we can afford to do without. Each has its proper purpose and use. Character, for its full formation, needs its winter as well as its springtime, and its storms and its zephyrs alike. The main thing is to see to it that, by wise and careful husbandry, we take good value out of each vicissitude in its time.

"There is no reason to doubt," says Bushnell, "that God, in framing the plan or system of His spiritual agencies, ordained fluctuations and changing types of spiritual experience, that He might at intervals take advantage of novelty in arresting and swaying the minds of men. These are the springtimes of His truth, otherwise in danger of uniform staleness. Thus He rouses the spiritual lethargy of men and communities, and sways their will to Himself, by aid of scenes and manifestations not ordinary or familiar. Nor is it anything derogatory to the divine agency in the case, that the spiritual spring cannot remain perpetual; for there is a progress in God's works, and He goes on through change and multiform culture to ripen His ends . . .

"Not that the Christian is allowed at some times to be less religious than at others. He is under God's authority, and bound by His laws, at all times: he must answer to God for each moment and thought of his life. His covenant oath consecrates all his life to God, and stipulates for no intermission of service. It is his duty and privilege ever to be filled with the Spirit: God will never leave His temple except He is driven away by profanation (blasphemy, desecration. Ed.). The Christian is as much under obligation at one time as at another, though not under obligation to be ever doing the same things. No intermission, no wavering or slackness is permitted him; nay, he is bound to increase, or gather strength in his religious principles, every day and hour of his existence. God favors and appoints different moods, or kinds, of religious interest, but not backslidings or declensions of religious principle. There are diversities of gifts, but the same Spirit. There are diversities of operations, but it is the same God Who worketh all and in all."

While thus guarding against the thought of the manifestations of the Welsh revival, with its high tension, being a permanent condition, we rejoice in it exceedingly as a notable recurrence of God's spiritual springtime. Let us dismiss at once the thought of spiritual declension being necessary between such periods: our Lord can always keep us filled with His Spirit and loyal to His cause; but let us hail most heartily this special display of His grace and power, and pray and labor for its extension over all the land.

Truly God has visited His people in Wales. It is not a question of one town being awakened, but of the whole principality being on fire. Profanity silenced, public houses deserted, theaters closed, betting books burned, football teams disbanded, police courts idle, family feuds pacified, old-standing debts paid, sectarianism and ecclesiasticism submerged, the family altar re-erected, and Bible study become a passion—it is certainly a wonderful record.

"This is the finger of God." Not only does it hold large place in the religious weeklies, but the chief Cardiff journals give columns to the revival each day, and some of the principal London papers give a full column every morning. It is "The Acts of the Apostles up to date," as Gipsy Smith says.

One is struck with the simple spontaneity of it all. There is no great outstanding instrument of blessing, and little of organization. An indefinable influence pervades the country, and awakes to action in the services through the mere reading of a passage, or the singing of a well-known hymn, or the inelegant prayer of a collier or a country maiden. The ministers, even when in sympathy, take little part: routine and system are tabooed, and prim sermons quite at a discount: the meetings, often prolonged through the whole night, seem to conduct themselves. "Disorder," one would say. But no: from all accounts it is clear that there is a controlling spiritual power that dominates and directs in all. Everywhere stress is laid upon the personality and operation of the Holy Ghost—"the Pure Spirit," as the name reads in Welsh.

This was a feature that specially appealed to a London journalist, who visited the scene of the revival one Sunday in December. "The most extraordinary thing about the meetings I attended," he writes, "was the extent to which they were absolutely without any human direction or leadership. 'We must obey the Spirit,' is the watchword of Evan Roberts, and he is as obedient as the humblest of his followers. The meetings open—after any amount of singing while the congregation is assembling— by the reading of a chapter or a psalm. Then it is go-as-you-please for two hours or more. And the amazing thing is that it does go, and does not entangle in what might seem to be inevitable confusion. Three-fourths of the meeting consists of singing. No one uses a hymn book. No one gives out a hymn. The last person to control the meetings in any way is Mr. Evan Roberts. People pray and sing, give testimony, exhort as the Spirit moves them. As a study of the psychology of crowds, I have seen nothing like it. You feel that the thousand or fifteen hundred persons before you have become merged into one myriad-headed but single-souled personality."

The new theology is swamped, and sectarianism reduced to its proper level. "There is one lesson," says *The Christian*, "to be learned from the revival in Wales, which it is to be hoped will not be overlooked by the Church of Christ, viz., the breaking down of the barriers of sect. The separating walls are in most cases built up only of nonessentials; but, unhappily, they frequently are strong enough to impede spiritual waves. When the floodtide of a great revival comes they are swept away, and men clasp hands in the common blessing and joy. Why should they ever be rebuilt? The necessary separation is that "unto the gospel of God" (Rom. 1:1).

The rise of the movement is associated with the name of Evan Roberts, a young Welshman of twenty-six years, who had left the coal pit to study for the ministry. Last September he received that baptism of the Spirit which he had been seeking for thirteen years, and, under Divine impulsion, suspended his studies and went to preach the gospel at his home. Artless, shy, and unassuming, discouraging any dependence on his personality, he points people beyond himself to the Divine Agent who is at work in the land; and the course of the revival seems in no way tied to the movements of the evangelist. No one speaks of him as an orator. Living in the sphere of the eternal realities, he talks simply of them in his native tongue, as a child might. For instance—"You desire an outpouring of the Holy Spirit in your district? Well, four conditions must be observed. They are essential—mark the word, *essential.*

"(1) Is there any sin in your past that you have not confessed to God? On your knees at once! Your past must be put away and cleansed.

"(2) Is there anything in your life that is doubtful—anything you cannot decide whether it is good or evil? Away with it! There must not be a trace of a cloud between you and God. Have you forgiven *everybody—everybody?* If not, don't expect forgiveness for your own sins: you won't get it.

"(3) Do what the Spirit prompts. Obedience—prompt, implicit, unquestioning obedience to the

Spirit. Better offend ten thousand friends than quench the Spirit of God.

"(4) A public confession of Christ as your Savior. There is a vast difference between profession and confession.

"You praise the Father, praise the Son; why don't you praise the Holy Spirit? You speak of Him as 'something!' The Spirit has been smothered in hundreds of our churches. Quench not the Spirit. When the fire burns, it purifies, and when purified you are useful in the work of God."

There arises the question, What is to be done with the fruits of this movement? "Bend the churches and save the people," has been one of its watchwords; and truly, from all accounts, the churches have been wonderfully bent. The Spirit of the Lord has broken up, as Rev. John M'Neill writes, "that which we value far too much—this deadly, dull, respectable formality that passes for Christian worship and Christian work." But, unless we are mistaken, the religious systems as a whole must be prepared for permanent transformation, and must seek to adapt and accommodate themselves to this new spirit of life. To attempt to organize the work into forced conformity to the old types, corking up the "new wine" in "old bottles," must be a fatal course. As Mr. Lloyd George, M. P., points out, in wishing God-speed to the revival, "The most important thing to urge in connection with it is that the religious leaders of Wales should see, in time, that the great forces which have been aroused into activity should not be wasted in mere outbursts of emotion. Let them in time overhaul their denominational machinery, and adapt it to the new and the greater demand upon its resources which has been created by this remark-able upheaval, which seems to be rocking Welsh life like a great earthquake."

This is no passing enthusiasm. The Welsh are poetical, but not hysterical; well informed, sober, intelligent. Their best moral and religious impulses in the past two centuries have sprung from movements such as this.

And there are evidences already that the revival is not to be merely local. The Welsh community in London is wakening, and there is a stirring of new life in some of the English countries. Mr. Roberts has Divine assurance that the movement is to be worldwide. Among ourselves there has been the impression that the special prayers of the past two years are about to be answered. Pilgrim Lyall's article of this month was prepared before the Welsh Revival was heard of. Unheard of was it also when the day of prayer for revival was announced in our October number. Is the answer to our prayers upon us?

We can not do better than close with Mrs. Penn-Lewis' words, "All that we read of this work in Wales

JESSIE PENN-LEWIS

must awaken a great longing in many hearts for such a movement of God all over Great Britain. Oh, that individual churches would suspend ordinary services, and appoint gatherings for prayer until the same Holy Spirit breaks forth in their midst! Does this seeking unto God in prayer not correspond to the ten days of prayer by the hundred and twenty before Pentecost, until the Holy Spirit came? Dr. John Smith pointed out at Keswick, that He is the Eternal Spirit 'which proceedeth'—*i.e.*, is eternally and ceaselessly proceeding—'from the Father' into the world. He is ready to pour into every soul, and every church, and every town, in answer to united prayer. He must and will respond, as He is honored and given His place among men. He is 'the Executive Power of the Godhead,' in charge of the Church of Christ on earth. He will manifest Himself as soon as He is recognized and given His place. '*Oh, Spirit of Burning, Come!*' "

Bright Words

REVIVAL PARAGRAPHS

Before the Revival—Rev. H. Elvet Lewis said that for some time his fellow ministers had been greatly concerned and almost heartbroken because of the manifest lessening of the hold which religion had upon the young people of their congregations. So-called "Ethical Societies" were drawing them away from their sanctuaries, and the publications of a rationalistic press were taking the place of the Word of God. Groups of men and women were praying for their young men, and the answer had come, not in the way they might have expected, but in God's own way.

Revival Excitement—"Let it not be suspected that we are afraid of all stir and excitement. The greatest and best actions have ever been performed in stages of excited feeling and high personal exaltation. Nothing was ever achieved in the way of great and radical changes in men or communities without some degree of excitement; and if anyone expects to carry on the cause of salvation by a steady rolling on the same dead level, and fears continually lest the axles wax hot and kindle into a flame, he is too timorous to hold the reins in the Lord's chariot."—*Bushnell*

Revival Awakes the Conscience—The Rev. J. J. Morgan, who was at tonight's meeting, tells me that at a chapel where he had just been preaching, one of the deacons read aloud to the congregation a letter from a member, acknowledging that years ago he kept back the price of some tickets sold for the church. He now returned the money, and humbly begged for forgiveness.—*Daily News*

Revival Revives the Memory—A still more striking indirect effect of the revival was told me by a gentleman at Hafod tonight. "Eight years ago," he said, "a lady borrowed a sovereign from my wife. When asked for it after a few weeks, she denied the debt. Now she has sent the sovereign back, acknowledging that her statement was a lie, and asking for forgiveness. This story would have a most sensational effect if I were permitted to reveal the lady's name and the position of her husband. For eight years this trifling debt has been rankling in her conscience.—*Daily News*

The Sun, Not the Stars—Deprecating the intrusion of General Booth and other eminent leaders upon the Welsh Revival, "Invicta" writes to the *Daily News*, "A revival without a famous orator! Can it be? Why, anyone almost can say as clever things as Evan Roberts if there were nothing but human cleverness in it. So there are thousands who quietly and trustfully are going to prayer on behalf of their own tiny churches and their own villages, that the Spirit which has come to Wales and found her ready by years of deep Scripture study and exercise of 'home religion,' may baptize these also.

"Let us plead, for the sake of the out-of-the-way workers that their rising hopes be not blighted by the fear lest after all it be of no use—that the work of God can only be done by the famous 'stars.' Let the stars rest awhile, that the Sun Himself may shine."

After Fifty Years—A few weeks ago the revival began at Hafod with an old collier of sixty-three years who had never been to a chapel service since he left Sunday school fifty years ago. His wife attended one of the missions of Mr. Evan Roberts at the neighboring town of Porth, and came home singing and praying. The next Sunday, while she was at the Silvan Chapel, of which she is a member, the old man came in and publicly gave himself up to Christ. His wife wept with joy, the congregation were moved to songs of passionate sympathy, the sermon had to be abandoned, and since then there have been no regular services, nothing but almost continuous revival.—*Daily News*

Revival Extravagance—It is very often true, when a revival seems to have an extreme character, that the fact is due, not to the real state produced, but to the previous fall, the death and desolation, with which it is contrasted. The dishonor does not belong to the revival, but to the decay of principle in the disciple which needs reviving. There ought to be no declension of real principle; but, if there is, no dishonor attaches to God in recovering His disciple from it, but the more illustrious honor. Commonly, if the ridicule were thrown upon the worldliness—the dishonorable looseness of life and principle—that preceded it, it would not be misplaced.—*Bushnell*

Not Abusive—Not a single word of abuse against any person or any class of the community found a place in the address of the revivalist or in the prayers of the congregation; and this consistent absence of any fierce tirade, which is too often part and parcel of the stock-in-trade of zealous propagandists, is one of the significant and most wholesome features of the present movement.—*Western Mail*, Cardiff

Christmas Revival—The Christ is asserting His claims in new and unexpected ways, and therein we do rejoice. Let materialistic men say what they will, the weeping and contrition of Welsh miners over sin, and its putting away by them, is more consonant with the true Christmas joy than all the empty songs and greetings of the multitudes who by their sin crucify afresh the Christ in the midst of their revelry.—Dr. Campbell Morgan

Blessed Fruits—Our young people desert the theater, the football field, and the public house by the thousand, and flock into every place of worship whose doors are open; and scores of them take part in every way they can to advance the movement. Old backsliders and hardened sinners follow the lead of the young, and come home rejoicing. Ministers of the gospel take heart and wait confidently. They all know the movement is of God, and are steadily preparing for the "building up which is to follow."—A Wales Minister

WELSH REVIVAL AND THE WESTERN MAIL

Perhaps the most extraordinary event in connection with the Welsh Revival has been the issue of "Revival Editions" of the Cardiff *Western Mail.* The last issue, published on Monday evening, has been forwarded to us, and is really a most remarkable achievement of modern journalism. Religious optimists have often dreamed of the time when revival news should take the place of racing and police court intelligence in the press; but here we have a whole evening paper given up bodily to reports of the progress of this marvelous spiritual movement. Our enterprising contemporary has set out the matter in the attractive form employed in the ease of ordinary news, with striking headlines, leaded type, and all the usual accessories of the evening paper. Instead of photographs of criminals and heroes of the football field, pictures of the evangelists are given, and a well-drawn cartoon illustrates the change in many a collier's home wrought at Christmas time through the agency of Mr. Evan Roberts.

On the back of the paper is printed a revival hymn set to music, and a summary of the conversions recorded since the beginning of the movement on November 8. Altogether the numbers have now reached 35,698—figures which represent a minimum estimate of the far-reaching character of the revival. The *Western Mail* has also issued a second pamphlet on the revival, bringing down the descriptions of the revival meetings to the end of last year. This pamphlet may be obtained at 176 Fleet Street, E. C., for one penny.

REPORT OF SPECIAL CORRESPONDENT IN *BELFAST WITNESS*

Reliable information from experienced Christian business men, well known in the metropolis, shows that the influence of the Welsh revival has been by no means overstated. Evidently the principality is stirred from end to end. Specially notable, perhaps, is the work at Barry, where the revival "has so far been carried on almost exclusively in connection with the Welsh churches, but its effect has been far-reaching. There is not a place of worship in the town—church and nonconformist alike—where the influence of the movement has not been felt. Special services have been held daily at different chapels at Barry, Barry Dock, and Cadoxton during the past week, and morning, noon, and night the congregations have been very large.

At the morning and afternoon meetings every day may be seen scores of instances of men who come home from work in the morning, attend the services during the day, and return to work again at night after but little rest. There has also been a considerable falling off in the attendance at the Technical School on the part of the young people, many of the boys and girls preferring to be present and take part in the revival services.

Already there have been over 300 public testimonies of conversion, and each gathering adds to this number. People walking up and down the streets resort almost unconsciously to hymn singing. Men and women who have lived openly lives of sin and indifference have come to the meetings—some, perhaps, from motives of curiosity, others to scoff and jeer—but have remained to pray, and, bathed in tears of sorrow and repentance, they have publicly declared their intention to forsake sin.

Last Sabbath, Gipsy Smith joined hands with Mr. Evan Roberts, at Mardy. Both spoke in the afternoon with pathos and power; yet the characteristic of the day was the perfect freedom of the meetings, the "harmony in confusion." Mr. Roberts said, "Don't talk about denominations these days" (bringing down

GIPSY SMITH

his hand on the pulpit stand). "Away with all that. Give us Christ; that is what we want," and there were responsive "Amens" from all parts of the chapel. Prayer followed prayer, the subdued character of the meeting being exceedingly impressive.

While a young supplicant was praying for the descent of the Spirit, and earnestly appealing for his friends to "seek Christ," a lady evangelist sang in an undertone, *I Need Thee Every Hour.* A young lady's prayers for "her brother who was in darkness" elicited a chorus of "Amens." Then a young man under the gallery, in evident distress, prayed, "Oh, God, I think you will forgive my sins. Oh, God, give me help to realize. Oh, God, give me faith. I have not been in the right spirit, and am weak." He then broke down, and the missioners hurried to him and prayed, while the congregation broke forth into *Diolch Iddo.* Another young man prayed in some-what similar terms. "The last words of my father were . . ." and his choking voice failed, and his sobs were drowned by the rendering of a stirring hymn. "The doors of the public houses are closed today," said one worshiper in prayer, "close them next week also."

The evening meeting was no less remarkable. Madame Kate Morgan-Llewelyn and Gipsy Smith took a prominent part, and Mr. Roberts was several times too overcome to take part. One young fellow, among other petitions, offered one for the local cy-cling club. Hymns and prayers followed, including what has now become a general favorite, *Tell Mother I'll Be There,* and this led Gipsy Smith to speak of his traveling to South Wales to see the lane in which his gypsy mother died in a gypsy tent. "We had no Bible then," he remarked. "But she found Him!" he added with a tone of triumph.

Mr. Roberts then essayed to speak. "I thought," he remarked, and his voice was almost choked with sobs, "when Gipsy Smith was talking about his mother having died in a tent—I thought of my Savior, who had no place whereon to lay His head, and . . ." He could proceed no further, and, overcome by emotion, he sobbed aloud. So affecting was the scene that the congregation was profoundly moved.

Belfast Witness

A QUICKENING AMONG ALL CLASSES

The great Welsh revival, which has attracted the attention of the Christian world, burst as a sudden flame of spiritual zeal, arousing thousands to concern over their salvation in addition to wonderfully moving professed Christians to seek the life more abundant. It seems to be a coincidence that, while Dr. Torrey is holding his great meetings with marked success in Great Britain, a special leader of the Welsh people should be raised up.

Evan Roberts, who has been largely instrumental in bringing about this revival, is a young man of only twenty-seven, and is described as not especially impressive in either appearance or speech, but as a man so completely consumed by his love for God and his anxiety to see men reconciled to their Father through Christ, that he fires with similar feeling multitudes with whom he is brought into contact.

The Welsh revival has known no class boundaries. Miners in the collieries have been converted by scores, old difficulties in labor circles are being healed, outdoor sports have been abandoned for the sake of attending the meetings, prayer meetings have been held even in barrooms, while proprietors of saloons have witnessed a great falling off in patronage. The Bishop of Llandaff came out in the press, bidding the movement Godspeed. The Salvation Army has been working among the lower classes, but the Warden of St. Michael's College declares that those are to be pitied for their ignorance who do not think that "respectable people" do not need to be reached by this remarkable movement.

Sectarian lines appear for the time to have been obliterated by this flood of power from on high that has lifted men above paltry bickering in their concern over the great question of coming into right relation with God.

As in such cases usually, the revival did not begin without much private prayer and preparation. Evan Roberts himself was so profoundly moved by the realization of God's love for men that his friends thought his reason in danger, and his landlady asked him to find another room. But when he began his work among the miners, he having once been a miner, it was soon evident that he was one of those who have been counted fools for Christ's sake, and that his seeming eccentricities were not the results of a disordered mind, but rather the manifestation of a soul so filled with Spirit-given power that it had to find a means of expending itself. The results promise to be both deep and lasting, and will be hailed by the devout everywhere as evidence that such seasons of awakening and quickening are not past, but may be brought about wherever there are men and women absolutely given up to such a purpose.

Union Gospel News

REPORT OF REV. F. B. MEYER: A MEMORABLE DAY IN WALES

F. B. MEYER

Leaving Paddington at 5:30 A. M., we reached Neath, in South Wales, about noon, and took a carriage for the mountain village of Llansamlct, about three and a half miles distant. There were no romantic views along the road—just collieries and straggling mining villages, where life bore the most monotonous and depressing aspect. Little wonder that men who live under such conditions crave strong excitements to lift them above their surroundings.

No money is spent on advertising the revival meetings, and there are no posters on the hoardings. No need to print Evan Roberts in large type in order to secure a crowd. It is the presence of the Holy Spirit in mighty power that attracts. Still the lack of direction is rather disconcerting to a stranger;

though, in our case, the difficulty was lessened by meeting groups of people hastening to the chapel, and we had the great pleasure of conveying thither the mother of the young miner student whom God has so greatly honored.

Mrs. Roberts is a happy woman today. She said that her step was much lighter than it used to be, and her heart is lighter. She told of the early years, when her husband broke his leg, and the lad had to go to the mine; and how, even then, he was different from other lads, had always a book in his hand, and cared for religion. She told how, before the revival came, he could neither eat nor sleep. Then the now familiar narrative of the outbreak of the revival at Loughor was told again; and then the account of the baptism which had come to her, after seeking it for eight days—"a kind of burning in my heart."

So we get to the little chapel, perched on those Welsh hills, the central building amid clustering cottages. It would seat about 600, and was filling fast. The area and galleries were soon packed with young miners, with women and girls, with men in the prime of life; two or three ministers in the big square pew below the pulpit; but no hymn books, no organ or piano—these were not needed to lead that magnificent singing, which rolled in successive billows of harmony over the congregation. What noble tunes! And the hymns full of the music of the gospel! Again and again you catch the names of Christ, of Golgotha, of Calvary! Such voices also, each trained to its part!

Two hours pass in prayers from old and young—from women for their husbands, from men for their mates—in singing, and in little snatches of exhortation but most of these are cut short, especially where the speaker is inclined to be prosy. Mr. McTaggart speaks a little in English, on the filling of the Holy Spirit; and there are one or two English choruses, as *For You I Am Praying* but the volume of sound is doubled when the congregation falls back again into the grand familiar sacred Welsh tongue, the language of childhood, of early memories, of sacred associations with the sainted dead.

Two or three young ladies quietly slip in, and take their seats beneath the pulpit; these accompany Mr. Roberts, and help by prayer, often broken with and ending in sobs, and with sweet solos, of which the people catch up and repeat the refrain. Presently Mr. Evan Roberts enters—a tall young man of twenty-seven years, with a pleasing open face, a winning smile, dark searching eyes, unobtrusive, simple, strong. No weakling this, but a man born to lead, and certain to be known as one of the great religious forces of the coming time! This is the man whom God has awakened to hold communion with Himself from 1 till 5 A. M. for three successive months, promising that a revival should break out, which like a tidal wave should sweep through the world. What wonder that he who has seen God is a master of assemblies, and that hearts bend before his words, though these may be the simplest!

Shortly after entering, he speaks a few words on the necessity of obeying the Spirit, which are interrupted, first by corroborating testimony on the part of two or three who feel impelled to bear witness, and then by bursts of song. The meeting next falls to prayer; and amongst others a young miner in the gallery mentions that some men behind him are mocking, and he prays for their conversion. Thereupon one of the men referred to gives the direct lie to the statement, and says that he is quite prepared to be convinced of the existence of God, if some tangible proof were given.

This challenge greatly agitated the meeting, and especially Mr. Evan Roberts, who cast himself on his knees, and began to wrestle for these two with the most terrible anguish of soul that I can conceive of. It was as though he were a father in agony for the life of his only son. His outcries were heartrending to listen to, and a friend of mine started a chorus to drown them. There was no effort at display, no unreality, no false emotionalism, but just travail of soul. Shame on us that so few have known it! That we have so callously considered the hardness of impenitent sinners! That our eyes have so seldom been fountains of tears! They told me afterwards that they were obliged to use a handkerchief to dry up the pool of tears upon the chair over which the revivalist bent.

After some time spent thus, he challenged the men to yield, and on their refusal he asked all the congregation to join him in prayer. In a moment every person in the place rose up, and knelt down; a hurricane of audible prayer swept through the place, and for some ten minutes the air was heavy with sobbing, strong crying, and prayers audibly uttered by 500 voices. I have heard nothing like it in my life. It reminded me of the piercing cry which arose to heaven when the Princess Alice went down with her living freight. A knot of people gathered round the two unyielding souls, and so we continued. Then Mr. Roberts called for an interval of silent prayer, and read the passage from *Exodus*, where the people are bidden to stand still and see God's salvation. It was one of the most moving spectacles that can be imagined, and it was impossible to speak for tears. What wonder that under such a strain of emotion two or three fainted, and had to be carried out; but these episodes were hardly noticed, and could not break the holy spell which was on all hearts.

IN THE SCHOOL OF THE HOLY GHOST

The meeting broke up at 5:30, and we hastened to the good minister's house (where the young revivalist was also staying) for a little hurried refreshment; and then, in the dark, along the muddy roads to the other chapel, Tabor, where the evening meeting was to be held. It was almost impossible to get in, but by great courtesy way was made for us. They recognized the London preacher, and urged him to speak, but he felt that his wisdom was silence before the great manifestation of Divine power, and that he must sit still as a little child in the school of the Holy Ghost.

For two hours the meeting took its Spirit-prompted course. A girl would pour out her heart in prayer, rising almost to agony; another would follow, falling at last into a kind of rhythmic chant; a minister would give a few words of exhortation; then a boy would pour out an earnest appeal for decisions, following his urgent words by dropping on his knees amid a group of his associates, and uttering his soul in prayer. So the time passes rapidly till Mr. Evan Roberts entered; and we, alas, must reluctantly tear ourselves away, pushing through the crowd to our carriage, and so back to the train. But we have seen and heard things which have unveiled the spirit-world, and are so totally dissimilar from the stereotyped religious forms that we are wont to pursue, as to usher us into a new world—should we not rather say into that old world which Pentecost introduced, and of which 1 Corinthians 12 is a specimen!

They who merely read such descriptions as this may think that the meetings are characterized by emotional excitement. But that is not the case. There are undoubtedly strong excitement and deep emotion, but these are well under control; and beneath all that can be accounted for by the influence of highly-exalted moods of soul on other minds, it is undeniable that the power of God is working after the fashion of those wonderful scenes of which our fathers have told us in 1859.

It is preeminently a young people's movement. Boys and girls, young men and women, crowd the chapels. The keynote is Calvary—no other aspect of the work of our Lord seems to satisfy. The personality and work of the Holy Spirit are in every prayer and on every tongue. The pent-up power of godly people which has too long been restrained, has broken loose, and before it the ministers are silenced. One told me that he felt that things would never again be as they had been in this direction, but that liberty of utterance would have to be conceded (during a part at least of the ordinary services) to the speech of the Holy Ghost through consecrated lips.

A new way of closuring the cranks and bores (silencing unwanted participants. Ed.), who have been the bane of our open meetings has been discovered in the power of sacred song; and an example has been set which may well be adopted universally. Of course there will have to be definite teaching, and even now I think there is room for more wise counsel than is for the most part permitted. But such things as these will necessarily right themselves as time goes on. In the meantime, there can be no doubt that God has answered prayer, and visited His people, and that the marvelous and widespread ethical results attest that this is the finger of God.

London Christian

REPORT BY R. A. TORREY

R. A. TORREY

Of course you have heard of the Welsh revival. The fire is breaking out throughout all South Wales, and now North Wales. It is manifestly God's work, not man's. A young man, Evan Roberts, who has received the baptism of the Holy Spirit, is quite prominent in some places, but there have been revivals in many towns where he has not gone at all, and often times there have been hundreds of conversions before he reaches the field. When he gets there he does not seem to try to run things in his own wisdom or strength. The meetings last for hours. Anyone speaks or sings that is so moved. Often times, even when Evan Roberts is speaking, some man or woman will burst out into a song, and he immediately stops speaking and lets the meeting take its own course. It bears a striking resemblance to the Irish revival of 1859, and also of what we read of the revival throughout America in 1857. The worldwide revival for which we have been praying seems to have begun. Let us thank God, but keep on praying.

One thing that especially cheers us about the work in Wales, is that at first we found Cardiff one of the hardest places to move that we have ever visited. I don't know that I have ever done so much scolding as I did there, trying to get the people to work, but when they woke up they woke up with all their hearts. We had a day of fasting and prayer, and prayed that God would kindle the fire throughout all Wales. This prayer is being answered, but unknown to us the fire had already broken out in different places. People are trying to tell where the revival began in Wales. One says it began in one place, and another in another. The truth is the fire broke out in different places quite independently of one another, in a sense, and yet in a deeper sense, not independently, for the same mighty Spirit of God was working in each place. I hope we may soon hear that in answer to the prayers of God's people in America, the fire is breaking out all over the land.

Sincerely yours,
R. A. Torrey

Lessons of the Welsh Revival

Sermon by the Rev. G. Campbell Morgan, D. D. Delivered in Westminster Chapel on Sunday Evening, 25th December, 1904

G. Campbell Morgan

"For these are not drunken, as ye suppose, seeing it is but the third hour of the day; but this is that which hath been spoken by the prophet Joel: And it shall be in the last days, saith God, I will pour forth of My Spirit upon all flesh: And your sons and your daughters shall prophesy, And your young men shall see visions, And your old men shall dream dreams: Yea, and on My bond-servants and on My bondmaidens in those days will I pour forth of My Spirit, and they shall prophesy" (Acts 2:15-18).

I have not read these words as a text, but as an introduction to what I desire to say, as God shall help me, concerning the most recent manifestation of the Pentecostal power. I refer to the great work of God that is going on in Wales at this time; and I trust that something more than curiosity makes you desire to hear of this work, for I am not speaking with any intention to satisfy curiosity. I want now in the simplest way to speak to you, first, very briefly, and as far as it is possible, of what my own eyes have seen, my own ears heard, and my own heart felt.

I do this in order that we may ask finally, what are the lessons God would teach us in this day of His visitation? Yet I can not help reverting, before going further, to the passage that I have read in your hearing. Peter stood in the midst of one of the most wonderful scenes that the world has ever beheld. When men said of the shouting multitude that they were drunk, Peter said, "No, these men are not drunken as ye suppose;" but "this is that" which was spoken by the prophet Joel. If any one shall say to me, "What do you think of the Welsh revival?" I say at once, "This is that."

This is no mere piece of imagination, and it certainly is not a piece of exaggeration. "I will pour forth of My Spirit upon all flesh, and your sons and your daughters shall prophesy," is the promise now evidently fulfilled in Wales. If you ask for proof of that assertion, I point to the signs. "Your young men shall see visions!" That is exactly what is happening. It does not at all matter that this cynical and dust-covered age laughs at the vision. The young men are seeing it. "And your old men shall dream dreams," and that is happening. The vision goes forward, the dream goes backward; and the old men are dreaming of '59, and feeling its thrill again. "Yea, and on My bond-servants and on My handmaidens," that is, on the slaves and the domestic servants, "I will pour My Spirit in those days; and they shall prophesy." It does not at all matter that some regular people are objecting to the irregular doings. "This is that." If you ask me the meaning of the Welsh revival, I say *it is Pentecost continued*, without one single moment's doubt.

But, for a few moments let me speak of the thing itself. Let me talk familiarly and quietly, as though sitting in my own room.

I left London on Monday, reaching Cardiff at 8:30 that evening, and my friend who met me said to me, "What are you going to do? Will you go home, or will you go to the meeting?" I said, "What meeting?" He said, "There is a meeting in Roath Road Chapel." "Oh," I said, "I would rather have a meeting than home." We went. The meeting had been going on an hour and a half when we got there, and we stayed for two hours and a half, and went home, and the meeting was still going on, and I had not then touched what is spoken of as—it is not my phrase, but it is expressive—the "fire zone." I was on the outskirts of the work. It was a wonderful night, utterly without order, characterized from first to last by the orderliness of the Spirit of God.

But it is of Tuesday that I would specially speak. I was the whole of that day in Clydach Vale; spending eight hours in the actual meetings, and the rest of the time in the company of Evan Roberts, whom God has so wonderfully raised up. When I had been to the evening meeting on Tuesday I told him I would not come back on Wednesday, and for reasons to be stated hereafter. Let me only say now in passing that I am perfectly convinced that we had better keep our hands off this work. I will explain that more fully presently. On Wednesday we returned to Cardiff, and, in answer to an invitation, Mr. Gregory Mantle and I took a meeting in this Roath Road Wesleyan Chapel, and on Thursday we took three meetings, spending seven hours there.

I want to speak of the Tuesday only. It was my holy privilege to come into the center of this wonderful work and movement. Arriving in the morning in the village, everything seemed quiet, and we wended our way to the place where a group of chapels stood. Oh, these chapels through Wales! Thank God for them! And everything was so quiet and orderly that we had to ask where the meeting was. And a lad, pointing to a chapel, said, "In there." Not a single person outside. Everything was quiet. We made our way through the open door, and just managed to get inside, and found the chapel crowded from floor to ceiling with a great mass of people. What was the occupation of the service? It is impossible for me to tell you finally and fully. Suffice it to say that throughout that service there was singing and praying, and personal testimony, but no preaching. The only break in upon the evidently powerful continuity of the service was when someone in the meeting, who happened to know me, said that they would like to hear me speak. And that is why I decided never to go again into these meetings. For the moment the thoughts of the meeting were turned towards me. There was a break in the continuity and the power. If it were possible for me in any way to disguise myself I would go back again, and get back into the middle of the movement, but I am afraid it is a little too late in the day for that. Of course I did not move to speak, but when, presently, it was evident that there was this break, I rose and spoke a few words, urging them not to allow the presence of any stranger to divert, their attention, and the meeting moved on, and I was allowed to hide myself again. It was a meeting characterized by a perpetual series of interruptions and disorderliness. It was a meeting characterized by a great continuity and an absolute order. You say, "How do you reconcile these things?" I do not reconcile them. They are both there. I leave you to reconcile them. If you put a man into the midst of one of these meetings who knows nothing of the language of the Spirit, and nothing of the life of the Spirit, one of two things will happen to him. He will either pass out saying, "These men are drunk," or he himself will be swept up by the fire into the kingdom of God. If you put a man down who knows the language of the Spirit, he will be struck by this most peculiar thing. I am speaking with diffidence, for I have never seen anything like it in my life; while a man praying is disturbed by the breaking out of song, there is no sense of disorder, and the prayer merges into song, and back into testimony, and back again into song for hour after hour, without guidance. These are the three occupations— singing, prayer, testimony. Evan Roberts was not present. There was no human leader.

Mr. Mantle was with me, and spoke a word or two, when a man in the gallery rose and said to him in broken English, "Is your work in London near Greenwich?" "Yes," said Mr. Mantle, "close to Greenwich." "Take this address down," said the man, "my brother is there. He is drinking and a skeptic. I am praying for him." Mr. Mantle pulled out his notebook, and said, "Give me the address," and he dictated it to him, and then they started singing

Songs of Praises, and the man prayed, and Mr. Mantle is on his track today. That is an incident. A most disorderly proceeding, you say? I will be very glad when that happens here, when you will break through all conventionalities. When a man is in agony about the soul of his brother, he will dare to ask. But it must only be as the spontaneous answer of the soul to the Spirit of God.

In the afternoon we were at another chapel, and another meeting, equally full, and this time— *Evan Roberts was present.*

He came into the meeting when it had been on for an hour and a half. I went with him, and with the utmost difficulty we reached the platform. I took absolutely no part, and he took very little part. He spoke, but his address—if it could be called an address—was punctuated perpetually by song and prayer and testimony. And Evan Roberts works on that plan, never hindering any one. As the result of that afternoon I venture to say that if that address Evan Roberts gave in broken fragments had been reported, the whole of it could have been read in six or seven minutes. As the meeting went on, a man rose in the gallery and said, "So and So," naming some man, "has decided for Christ," and then in a moment the song began. They did not sing *Songs of Praises*, they sang *Diolch Iddo*, and the weirdness and beauty of it swept over the audience. It was a song of praise because that man was born again. There are no inquiry rooms, no penitent forms, but some worker announces, or an inquirer openly confesses Christ, the name is registered, and the song breaks out, and they go back to testimony and prayer.

In the evening exactly the same thing. I can tell you no more, save that I personally stood for three solid hours wedged so that I could not lift my hands at all. That which impressed me most was the congregation. I looked along the gallery of the chapel on my right, and there were three women, and the rest were men packed solidly in. If you could but for once have seen the men, evidently colliers, with the blue seam that told of their work on their faces, clean and beautiful. Beautiful, did I say? Many of them lit with heaven's own light, radiant with the light that never was on sea and land. Great rough, magnificent, poetic men by nature, but the nature had slumbered long. Today it is awakened, and I look on many a face, and I knew that men did not see me, did not see Evan Roberts, but they saw the face of God and the eternities. I left that evening, after having been in the meeting three hours, at 10:30, and it swept on, packed as it was, until an early hour next morning, song and prayer and testimony and conversion and confession of sin by leading church members publicly, and the putting of it away, and all the while no human leader, no one indicating the next thing to do, no one checking the spontaneous movement.

Now, for one moment let me go a step further and speak just a word or two about the man himself. Evan Roberts is hardly more than a boy, simple and natural, no orator, no leader of men; nothing of the masterfulness that characterized such men as Wesley, and Whitefield, and Moody: no leader of men. One of our most brilliant writers in one of our morning papers said of Evan Roberts, in a tone of sorrow, that he lacked the qualities of leadership, and the writer said if but some prophet did now arise he could sweep everything before him. God has not chosen that a prophet shall arise. It is quite true. Evan Roberts is no orator, no leader. What is he? I mean now with regard to this great movement. He is the mouthpiece of the fact that there is no human guidance as to man or organization. The burden of what he says to the people is this: It is not man, do not wait for me, depend on God, obey the Spirit. But whenever moved to do so, he speaks under the guidance of the Spirit. His work is not that of appealing to men so much as that of creating an atmosphere by calling men to follow the guidance of the Spirit in whatever the Spirit shall say to them.

I do not hesitate to say that God has set His hand upon the lad, beautiful in simplicity, ordained in his devotion lacking all the qualities that we have looked for in preachers and prophets, and leaders. He has put him in the forefront of this movement that the world may see that He does choose the things that are not to bring to naught the things that are, the weak things of the world to confound the things that are mighty; a man who lacks all the essential qualities which we say make for greatness, in order that through him in simplicity and power He may move to victory.

For a moment let us stand back, and look at the whole thing more generally. Let me speak of some of the incidental peculiarities of the movement as I saw it, and gathered information concerning it on the ground. In connection with the Welsh revival there is no preaching, no order, no hymn books, no choirs, no organs no collection, and, finally, no advertising. Now, think of that for a moment, again, will you? Think of all our work I am not saying these things are wrong. I simply want you to see what God is doing. There were the organs, but silent the ministers, but among the rest of the people, rejoicing and prophesying with the rest, only there was no preaching. Yet, the Welsh revival is the revival of preaching to Wales. Everybody is preaching. No order, and yet it moves from day to day, week to week, county to county with matchless precision, with the order of an attacking force. No books, but, ah me, I nearly wept tonight over the singing of our last hymn. Mr. Stead was asked if he thought the revival would spread to London, and he said, "It depends upon whether you can sing." He was not so wide of the mark. When these Welshmen sing, they sing the words like men who believe them. They abandon themselves to their singing. We sing as though we thought it would not be respectable to be heard by the man next to us. No choir, did I say? It was all choir. And hymns! I stood and listened in wonder and amazement as that congregation on that night sang hymn after hymn, long hymns, sung through without hymn books. Oh, don't you see it? The Sunday school is having its harvest now. The family altar is having its harvest now. The teaching of hymns and the Bible among those Welsh hills and valleys is having its harvest now. No advertising. The whole thing advertises itself. You tell me the press is advertising it. I tell you they did not begin advertising it until the thing caught fire and spread. And let me say to you, one of the most remarkable things is the attitude of the Welsh press. I come across instance after instance of men converted by reading the story of the revival in the *Western Mail* and the *South Wales Daily News.*

WHAT IS THE ORIGIN OF THE MOVEMENT?

In the name of God let us all cease trying to find it. At least let us cease trying to trace it to any one man or convention. You cannot trace it, and yet I will trace it tonight. Whence has it come? All over Wales—I am giving you roughly the result of the questioning of fifty or more persons at random in the week—a praying remnant has been agonizing before God about the state of the beloved land, and it is through that the answer of fire has come. You tell me that the revival originates with Roberts. I tell you that Roberts is a product of the revival. You tell me that it began in an endeavor meeting where a dear girl bore testimony. I tell you that was part of the result of a revival breaking out everywhere. If you and I could stand above Wales, looking at it, you would see fire breaking out here, and there, and yonder, and somewhere else, without any collusion or prearrangement. It is a Divine visitation in which God—let me say this reverently—in which God is saying to us: See what I can do without the things you are depending on; see what I can do in answer to a praying people; see what I can do through the simplest, who are ready to fall in line, and depend wholly and absolutely upon Me.

What is the character of this revival? It is a church revival. I do not mean by that merely a revival among church members. It is that, but it is held in church buildings. Now, you may look astonished, but I have been saying for a long time that the revival which is to be permanent in the life of a nation must be associated with the life of the churches. What I am looking for is that there shall come a revival breaking out in all our regular church life. The meetings are held in the chapels, all up and down the valleys, and it began among church members, and when it touches the outside man it makes him into a church member at once. I am tremendously suspicious of any mission or revival movement that treats with contempt the church of Christ, and affects to despise the churches. Within five weeks *20,000 have joined the churches.*

I think more than that have been converted, but the churches in Wales have enrolled during the last five weeks 20,000 new members. It is a movement in the church, and of the church, a movement in which the true functions and forces of the church are being exercised and filled.

Now, what effect is this work producing upon men? First of all, it is turning Christians everywhere into evangelists. There is nothing more remarkable about it than that, I think. People you never expected to see doing this kind of thing are becoming definite personal workers. Let me give you an illustration. A friend of mine went to one of the meetings, and he walked down to the meeting with an old friend of his, a deacon of the Congregational Church, a man whose piety no one doubted, a man who for long years had worked in the life of the church in some of its departments, but a man who never would think of speaking to men about their souls, although he would not have objected to some one else doing it. As my friend walked down with the deacon, the deacon said to him, "I have eighteen young men in an athletic class of which I am president. I hope some of them will be in the meeting tonight." There was a new manifestation. Within fifteen minutes he left his seat by my friend and was seen talking to a young man down in front of him. Presently the deacon rose and said, " Thank God for So and So," (giving his name) " he has given his heart to Christ right here." In a moment or two he left him, and was with another young man. Before that meeting closed that deacon had led every one of those eighteen young men to Jesus Christ, who never before thought of speaking to men about their souls.

My own friend, with whom I stayed, who has always been reticent of speaking to men, told me how, sitting in his office, there surged upon him the great conviction that he ought to go and speak to another man with whom he had done business for long years. My friend suddenly put down his pen, and left his office, and went on 'Change, (abbreviation for "exchange," a place where merchants meet. Ed.) and there he saw the very man, and going up to him, passing the time of day to him, the man said to him, "What do you think of this revival?" And my friend looked him squarely in the eye and said, "How is it with your own soul?" The man looked back at him, and said, "Last night at twelve, from some unknown reason, I had to get out of bed and give myself to Jesus Christ and I was hungering for some one to come and talk to me." Here is a man turned into an evangelist by supernatural means. If this is emotional, then God send us more of it! Here is a cool, calculating business ship owner, that I have known all my life, leaving his office to go on 'Change, and ask a man about his soul.

Another characteristic is that you never know just where this fire is going to break out next. A preacher in one of the towns down there said, "I have got a sermon in my pocket. It has been there for three weeks. I went down to my church three Sundays ago with a sermon prepared, my notes in my pocket, and that morning some man broke out in testimony, and it was followed by prayer and singing, and it has never ceased, but two hundred people have joined the church." He said, " I am keeping that sermon!"

The other day—down in one of the mines—and I hope you understand! I am only repeating to you the instances that came under my personal observation—the other day in one of the mines, a collier was walking along, and he came, to his great surprise, to where one of the principal officials in the mine was standing. The official said, "Jim, I have been waiting two hours here for you."

"Have you, sir?" said Jim. "What do you want?" "I want to be saved, Jim." The man said, "Let us get right down here," and there in the mine, the colliery official, instructed by the collier, passed into the kingdom of God. When he got up he said, "Tell all the men, tell everybody you meet, I am converted." Straightway confession.

The horses are terribly puzzled. A manager said to me, "The haulers are some of the very lowest. They have driven their horses by obscenity and kicks. Now they can hardly persuade the horses to start working, because there is no obscenity and no kicks." The movement is characterized by the most remarkable confession of sin, confessions that must be costly. I heard some of them, men rising who have been members of the church, and officers of the church, confessing hidden sin in their heart, impurity committed and condoned, and seeking prayer for its putting away. The whole movement is marvelously characterized by a confession of Jesus Christ, testimony to His power, to His goodness, to His beneficence, and testimony merging forevermore into outbursts of singing.

Now let us stand back a little further and speak of the essential notes, as I have noticed some of the incidental peculiarities. I say to you today, beloved, without any hesitation, that this whole thing is of God, that it is a visitation in which He is making men conscious of Himself, without any human agency. The revival is far more widespread than the fire zone. In this sense you may understand that the fire zone is where the meetings are actually held, and where you feel the flame that burns. But even when you come out of it, and go into railway trains, or into a shop, a bank, anywhere, men everywhere are talking of God. Whether they obey or not is another matter. There are thousands who have not yielded to the constraint of God, but God has given Wales in these days a new conviction and consciousness of Himself. That is the profound thing, the underlying truth.

And then another essential note to be remembered is this. I have already said that it is essentially a church revival in the broadest sense of that word. What is the church doing? If you go to Wales and get near this work you will see the church returning to the true functions of her priesthood. What are the functions of the Christian priesthood? Of course I need hardly stay to say that I am referring to the priesthood of the church, for there is no priesthood in the church separated from the church; and I am not at all sure that God is not restoring to Wales the true functions of priesthood, partly because she refuses to be dominated by any false system of priesthood. There are two essential functions to the Christian priesthood. The first is Eucharistic, the giving of thanks; the other is intercessory praying. That is all that is going on. The church everywhere singing and praying and offering praise, and pleading with God. Every meeting is made up almost exclusively of these things. Evan Roberts, and those who sing with him, and those who are speaking in other parts are urging the people to praise, to pray, and the church everywhere is doing it; and while the church is praising, singing plaintively in Welsh such songs as:

> "Oh, the Lamb, the gentle Lamb,
> The Lamb of Calvary,"

Or, while the church is singing of the love of God, men and women are coming down broken hearted, sin convicted, yielding themselves to Jesus Christ. It is a great return on the part of the church, under the inspired touch of the Spirit of God, to the exercise of its priestly functions—giving praise and interceding.

And then it is a great recognition of the presence and power of the Spirit manifesting itself in the glorification of Christ. What are the effects produced upon the converts?

Again I am taking the largest outlook. Two words, I think, cover the whole thing—vision and virtue. Men are seeing things! Oh, yes, it is quite cheap and easy to stay at a distance and smile. It is intensely easy for the *Lancet* to predict insanity. I will tell you something in passing. The insanity that will be produced in Wales by this Welsh revival will be as nothing to the insanity from drink which it will cure.

It is intensely cheap and easy for cold-blooded men at a distance, who know nothing of Celtic fire or spiritual fire, to smile at this whole thing, this seeing of visions. But while you smile, these men are seeing visions. They will tell you crudely of them, perhaps, but it is one of those strange things that no man can ever tell of a vision when he sees it really. They are seeing God. Well, but you say that will pass. It is passing. The vision is passing out into virtue, and men are paying their debts, and abandoning the public house, and treating their horses well. Oh, my masters! Did you say the next revival would be ethical? It is that, because it is spiritual, and you will never get an ethical revival except in this way. Vision is merging into virtue, and theatrical companies are packing up and going back because there are no houses, and on every hand there is sweeping down these Welsh valleys a great clean river. It is the river of God, and men are being cleansed in it, in personal and civic relationships. We are quite willing to appeal to the coming years about this work, but the evidences are already present on every hand. Tradesmen are being startled by men paying debts even though the statute of limitations has run out. Tradesmen, you know what that means! An emotion that will make a man do that is worth cultivating and it is good all the way through.

This is very fragmentary, but it must be if a man talks of these things. No man ever yet could describe a burning bush, and I know I have not described this to you.

Will you let me hold you while I say something to you about our own lessons?

First of all as to Wales itself, and especially to this great district, I am perfectly sure that it will be a good thing for us if we let it alone. By that I mean that General Booth never manifested his wisdom more than when he packed up and came home. And I love him, and have for years. Any of us that go down there with any thought in our heart we can help, we had better leave the thing in God's hand. To me it is so sacred a manifestation and glorious that I became frightened, as it wore on, lest my presence, without any desire that it should be so, should check the great movement. That was why I said to Evan Roberts, "I am going away, man, because I will not, so help me God, hinder by five minutes this great work." I feel we had better let that thing run. We did not originate it anywhere, and—forgive the Americanism—we cannot run it. We had better stand aside and pray, and get ready for what God means to do for us.

What are the great values of this movement in Wales? First, the reaffirmation of the spiritual. Secondly, this marvelous union of the spiritual with the practical, this manifestation of an ethical result from a spiritual renewal. Let me say it, I am not at all sure that God is not rebuking our over-organization. We certainly have been in danger of thinking there could not be a revival, or any work done for God, unless we had prepared everywhere. I am the last man to speak against organization in its proper place, but I am inclined to think God is saying to us, "Your organizations are right, providing you do not live in them, and end in them." But here, apart from all of them, setting them almost ruthlessly on one side, Pentecostal power and fire are being manifested.

What shall we do in the presence of this great movement? Imitate it? Imitation will be fatal. Let no man come back and attempt to start anywhere in

London meetings on the lines of those held in Wales, and for this simple reason that no man started them there. If somewhere here there should break out some great manifestation such as this, then God grant we be ready to fall in line. You cannot imitate this kind of thing. What shall we do? If we cannot imitate, we can discover the principles. What are they? Let us listen for the Spirit, confess Christ, be absolutely at His disposal. Oh, but you say to me, Are not we all that? Well, I do not know. God help us to find out for ourselves. I think we are in terrible danger of listening to the Spirit, and when His voice speaks to us, quenching Him. You say, Something moved me to speak to that man about his soul, but I did not like to. That is how revival is stopped. Speak to him. Listening to the Spirit, confessing Christ openly; absolutely at His disposal.

Let us in our church work not attempt to imitate the thing afar, but let us prayerfully take hold of every organization and every method, and strengthen it. Strengthen it how? By seeing to it that through the organization the Spirit of God has right of way by bringing your Sunday school class, dear teacher, into a new realm, and instead of treating it as a company of boys and girls who care for very much, that you teach and interest on Sunday afternoons, treat it as a company of souls to be saved. Begin to try and teach along that line, instead of treating our congregations as congregations to be instructed ever in holy things treat them as men and women that are to be persuaded to holy things, and consecration, and Jesus Christ. And in order to the doing of all this, what we supremely need is that we ourselves should be at the end of ourselves, that we should dare to abandon ourselves with some amount of passion to our work. Oh, we have been too—

"Icily regular, faultily faultless,
Splendidly null."

What we do need is the abandonment of ourselves to the great truths we know so well, to the great forces that indwell. Let us "strengthen the things that remain."

And so—now forgive me if I address myself to my own people—shall we not turn ourselves—ministers and staff and officers, and all the members, and shall we not say, at least we can now take up this work and make it instinct with new devotion and life, at least we can take hold of the thing that lies closest, and put into it the passion of a great devotion. We can begin there. The church of God needs three things.

It needs first to set itself to get things out of the way for God. I appreciate the almost puzzled look upon some of your faces. What things? I do not know. All the things that are in His way: Your habit that you know is unholy; your method of business that will not bear the light of day; your unforgiving heart towards a church member. Oh, God forgive me that I mention anything! You know, you know. They are in God's way, these things. They must be cleared out. That is the first thing. There may be other things in God's way. Any organization in church life that does not make for the salvation of men is a fungous growth, and the sooner we drop it off the better. Oh, I know churches where classrooms are so tremendously full there is no room for a prayer meeting. Are we ready to put things out of the way for God? I think we are. I think that if God manifests

Himself, and men begin to be saved, I do not think there is a guild social we will keep. I do not think there is any bazaar coming on that will hinder it! Oh, if there is anything, we must be prepared to sweep everything out for God to have highway. That is the attitude the church must be prepared to take.

Now let me say also to the other churches, that is the true attitude. There is nothing so important as the saving of men, and when the church says that, and is ready, God will come. We need then to wait upon Him in earnest constant prayer.

Oh, brothers, sisters, pray, pray alone; pray in secret, pray together; and pray out of a sense of London's sin and sorrow. It is so easy to be familiar with these things, until they have lost their power to touch us. Oh, the sin and the sorrow of London! May God lay it upon our hearts as a burden. And out of that agony let us begin to pray, and go forward the moment He opens the door, and indicates the way. I do not expect—and especially to young Christians do I say this—I do not expect just the same kind of manifestation. God always manifests Himself through the natural temperament, and you can never have the poetic fire and fervor of a Celtic revival in London. But you can have a stern, hard, magnificent consecration, and results that characterize your own nationality. Are we ready for God? I feel like apologizing to you tonight for this broken talk. I have talked out of my heart. I have tried to talk of fire that cannot be described. I have tried to talk out of the tremendous sense that God is abroad, and I talk out of the desire that I can not express—that somewhere, some when, somehow, He may put out His hand, and shake this city for the salvation of men.

Selections from English Papers

The Revival at Carnarvon

Last week you published a most readable account of the revival at Talvsarn, Carnarvonshire, and it may interest your readers to know something about the movement in Carnarvon, the capital of North Wales.

Carnarvon is the most Welsh of all the Welsh towns; it is Nonconformist to the core, and can boast some of the largest chapels in the northern part of the principality; but, in spite of all the facilities it possesses, a great bulk of the inhabitants were altogether indifferent towards all things religious, and the places of worship on Sundays were poorly attended. None but the faithful went to the weeknight prayer meetings, and often there would not be more than a dozen or two present at each chapel.

A wonderful change has come over the scene within the last fortnight or so. Prayer meetings, which were never so popular, are held nightly—and often twice daily—in all the chapels, and they are attended by young and old, rich and poor, and many are the converts. The young people seem to take greater interest in the meetings than the grown ups, and the revival, so far as Carnarvon is concerned, may be said to be the result of an awakening among the young people of the town. The conversation of boys in the streets turns upon the revival, and it is nothing unusual to hear one asking the other if he is going to the prayer meeting. The services are throughout spontaneous, resembling a Quakers' meeting, and at a Congregational Chapel a few miles from Carnarvon, a boy of fourteen years went forward to the big pew to pray. He asked the Lord to forgive his sins, saying that he had been in the habit of reciting verses from Scripture in chapel on Sunday evenings, and afterwards smoking cigarettes and swearing. He declared that from that day on he would never do it again, and that he was going to lead a new life. This is but one instance of the effect the revival has had upon the young people.

Young men and women—whose voice had never before been heard at a public gathering of any kind—take part freely in the meetings, and some remarkable scenes have been witnessed. On Sunday night last at Pendlref Congregational Chapel—the oldest chapel in the town—four young women prayed so impressively and so earnestly that many in the large congregation were moved to tears. One old backslider overcome with emotion, appealed to the people to pray that he might receive strength to resist temptation and to lead a better life. Thereupon a young woman rose in the body of the chapel and prayed fervently for him, and afterwards the congregation broke out into singing the well-known hymn, *Diolch iddo byth am gofio llwch y llawr.*

An intense feeling of devotion permeated the meeting, which will be long remembered by those who had the privilege to be present. Two men who had followed afar off for many years gave themselves up to Christ, and the same night, at other chapels in the town, there were many converts. Prayer meetings are being held this week again, and by request all the shops are closed at an earlier hour than usual to enable shop assistants and others to attend the meetings. The revival has already purified the moral atmosphere of the town. The public houses are losing their customers—the people think of nothing but prayer meetings—and drunkenness in the streets is becoming a rare occurrence.

A strange place wherein to hold a prayer meeting is certainly a railway carriage, yet this is what took place on the railway near Carnarvon the other day. In the quarries at Llanberis and Nantlee Vale prayer meetings are held daily by the men during the dinner hour. There was a time when the quarrymen could not get their dinner over soon enough to play cards, but now they want to finish their dinner as quickly as possible in order to participate in the prayer meetings.

From the villages surrounding Carnarvon reports come of most excellent meetings, and the converts are many.

British Weekly

Remarkable Scene in a Coal Mine

While in the Mid-Glamorgan district last week I spent a few hours in the Llynvi Valley, which so far has not been visited by Evan Roberts. However, the whole valley is aflame with the revival spirit, and wonderful scenes are being witnessed both above and under ground. At the invitation of the manager of the Coegnant pit, one of North's Navigation Collieries near Nantyffyllon, I descended the pit at six o'clock the other morning. Reaching the bottom,

I walked along the "partings" till I reached the "Baltic" seam. My guide, after explaining the workings of the mine, piloted me to a recess in this seam where

A Typical Welsh Miner with a Davy Lamp from the Revival Period.

a number of colliers had assembled. Presently the numbers increased, till over three hundred men, each with his safety lamp, were gathered in a strange crowd. Some were seated on the floor; others knelt, and numbers were standing. One of the number struck up *Diolch Iddo* (*Thanks be to Him*); this was taken up by the others, and repeated again and again. An old collier jumped up, and told in Welsh how after five unsuccessful attempts to get a fellow-workman to give his heart to God he had at the sixth attempt the previous night triumphed. *Diolch Iddo* again rang through the galleries. Two men prayed simultaneously, one in English and one in Welsh. Before they had finished, from the far end of the seam came the strains—in a rich bass voice— of *Guide Me, O Thou Great Jehovah*. In a moment everybody present was singing this beautiful hymn. Never did it sound so impressive as deep down in the bowels of the earth that morning. A dozen colliers of all ages testified at once, and prayer followed prayer in quick succession, when in a truly "encircling gloom," the men sang *Lead, Kindly Light,* many of them swinging their lamps; one marveled at this great change that had come over these men whose usual occupation before starting work was singing comic songs and indulging in coarse jest and vulgarity. The ponies walking between the curve lines on their way to the workings seemed amazed at the strange sounds and scenes. A brief address in Welsh was delivered by one of the men, who appealed for those who were on their way to glory to show lamps. Hundreds were hoisted aloft, and a few remained on the ground. The owners of the latter were immediately objects of pity and prayer. All went on their knees and sang, *For You I Am Praying,* and as it was time to commence work, the benediction was pronounced, the men marching to their work, singing, *Throw Out the Life Line.* Mr. David Davis, the manager of this pit, told me he had not heard one of the men swear for over three weeks a remarkable thing indeed. This scene is only one, typical of many that are daily taking place in South Wales coal mines, and at which many men are being converted.

Help from the Established Church

As to the Welsh revival and its results, our Cardiff correspondent telegraphs that the movement for removing friendly society gatherings from public houses to other premises has resulted in definite action at Treorky. At Six Bells, in the Valley of Monmouth, the converts under Mr. Sidney Evans' ministry, include the captain of a tug-of-war team, who rose and said that he had been a "waster for sixteen years," and that people now said he was mad. "Thank God, I shall have heaven for my asylum, and Christ for my keeper," he replied.

A Pontypridd student has gone to Worcester to conduct a mission. Pembrokeshire is also being leavened with the same spiritual intensity, and at a Pembroke Dock service a father was so affected by the surrender of his son that he also joined the converts. In Cardiff the work continues, and a converted gambler thrilled all hearts by his account of how he was about to cast himself into the Thames when thoughts of his mother checked him.

The established church is daily becoming more closely linked with the revival. One of those who has aided Mr. Roberts is the Rev. F. T. Webster, of All Souls', Langham Row, London.

Beyond question, the church and nonconformity in these counties have got into closer and kindlier contact since the revival. This week it was a unique sight to see the clergyman of a parish voluntarily take second place at a burial service, the whole of the service within the church being conducted by a Baptist minister.

Mr. Jones, pastor of Moriah Chapel, Loughor, where the revival fire first kindled, has resigned, practically as a protest against the late hours of the services. Mr. Jones believes the services should be shortened. For the sake of the young people they should not, he says, go beyond 9 or 10 P.M.

The most remarkable mission seen in the Potteries for many years has concluded at Hanley. Gipsy Smith announced that during the mission 1,500 people had been converted, and over 600 temperance pledges had been taken.

REPORTS BY MINISTERS IN BRITISH WEEKLY
THE REV. G. PENAR GRIFFITHS, SILOAM CONGREGATIONAL CHURCH, PENTRE, SWANSEA

"I must confess that I find myself amazed at the great and glorious change which has come over my dear old land and nation in such a short period, because change it is, with the Divine Hand effecting it. For some time I kept a watchful eye, and felt rather doubtful of the spontaneity of the movement; and not until I had spent two hours in one of the most inspiring meetings at Gorseinon did I come to believe that it was from above. I spent four more hours in that wonderful meeting, leaving the chapel and the crowd at one o'clock in the morning, never to question for a minute who had kindled this fire in the heart of my dear people. Divine! Yes, like the rainbow in Revelation. Think with me of the results in this order.

"1. *General Aspects*—We have very much more quiet in our streets, homes, works, and public places. The language of the people is greatly improved. To compare with what we had been accustomed to, we seldom hear foul language, where nothing but the foulest of it was used a few weeks ago. A tone of sincerity and great seriousness has possessed the people, as if they had at last realized the importance of life. At the same time, it is not sadness that reigns. There is a deep sense of joy real joy to be found where frivolity and indifference prevailed before.

"2. *Christian Spirit*—In this we have witnessed things which are miracles of grace. I personally know people who had been confirmed enemies, and for many years, to have sat down prayerfully to write letters seeking one another's forgiveness. Enemies have embraced each other in public services. People remembered their old debts to tradesmen, and hasten to pay them. The fever heat of worldliness has ceased to burn on the brow in the coal pit and in the market. Severe masters talk to their men, and deal with them more kindly. Conscience asserts itself more decidedly in capital and labor.

"3. *Conversions*—All over our land is spread abroad news of hundreds upon hundreds being saved. The scenes which we have witnessed baffle all description.

"4. *Church Life*—Here the influence is quite as strong, to say the least. People throng to chapels on Sundays and weekdays. There is the greatest readiness to take part in the service. No one need be asked to pray or speak; people get up uninvited. But, sir, what amazes me as much as anything is the wonderful aptitude displayed by each. Men and women, young men and maidens who had never before engaged in any public service, pray and speak with wonderful propriety. This is really a thing to wonder at; and the new ideas—ideas that were never expressed before they could be quoted by the dozens. Oh! it is wonderful. Lend me your good old *British Weekly* to say that I thank the Lord for being spared to see it. We have all ceased to be shy for Jesus Christ. We have passionate interest in men.

"Will the results be lasting? Yes. Because (1) it is the young man's revival; (2) the Bible is resorted to more than ever; (3) it has given us the very thing we were eagerly searching through all the years—joy. It is sanctified joy. At last we have had it in its highest form."

THE H. CERNYW WILLIAMS, CORWEN, EX-PRESIDENT OF THE WELSH BAPTIST UNION

"In reply to your inquiry, I can say that, so far as the revival has affected our church, it has been a great blessing. The same may be said of other churches in the town and district. It is a common sight now to see the chapels crowded at a prayer meeting. The absent Thomases are once more in their places, where they meet the risen Savior with His benedictions. The slow of speech have become eloquent, and the timid have grown bold. Those who have been praying in secret for some time venture to pray in public, and the careless and indifferent have been thoroughly roused.

"Some of us have been expecting a revival for some time, and had predicted when it came that it would affect the young people, and so it has, so that much latent power has been developed.

"Many pledges have been taken, and it is largely a temperance reformation. I believe the utmost care should be taken to guard against the perils connected with the movement. Meetings should not on any consideration be prolonged until very late, and we ought to see to it in time that this new force should be utilized for righteousness and truth. Converts must be directed to desire the sincere milk of the Word, that they may grow thereby."

THE REV. J. P. DAVIES,
TONYEFLIN BAPTIST CHURCH, CAERPHILLY

"Replying to your kind inquiry respecting the results of the 'Welsh revival,' I have much pleasure in stating that in my opinion it is thoroughly genuine, and carries with it all the marks of the Divine afflatus breath of the Spirit. Ed.). It has been the means of awakening and arousing the members of Tonyeflin to greater activity, and of filling them with more zeal for Christ and His work.

"I have vivid memories of the revival of 1859-60. The present one is quite, not to say more, as fervent, deep, and real. No doubt the movement is of God. I can not approve of everything connected with it, but I say may God speed it, and may it be wafted on the divine breeze to other countries.

"Very many new converts have been made, backsliders have been reclaimed, and a large number of new members have been added to my church, as well as other churches of the town and neighborhood."

THE REV. JOHN T. JOB,
CARNEDDI C. M. CHURCH, BETHESDA

"The revival has been the means of infusing a new spirit—a spirit of consecration in the service of Christ— into the churches of this district. It is felt already as a breath of love from on high amongst us, real and divine; and among its results the spirit of enmity between workmen and families, caused by the bitter quarry strife, gives way. Oh! the grandeur, the gentleness, yea, the sweet reasonableness of divine love! Verily, it is a pleasure to live here now. 'The society' in each church is blossoming as a rose under the breath of a heavenly spring. Truly, Christ is come to His garden once more among us. The vast majority of our people are churchgoing, and are, with only a few exceptions, enrolled members already. Hence we can not expect very many new converts here; still, about fifty have joined the churches already. A scene never to be forgotten was witnessed in Carneddi Church the other night, when a young man of about thirty-two got up and said he desired to give himself anew as a 'member.' 'The love of Christ constrained him to do so,' he said, although he enjoyed that privilege already. Would that such instances were multiplied generally throughout the churches of the land. What is this, I ask, but a true revival within the church itself? And when Zion putteth on 'her beautiful garments' the unbelief of the world will soon vanish away. We still expect greater things. The death of the cross is gradually conquering the young people of the district; they already, in hundreds, put forth pinions and rush like eagles to bask in the divine sunshine. The women's weekday prayer meeting, of some 500 strong, is held every afternoon without a break; and it has been without an exception a veritable Mount of Transfiguration, the scenes being indescribable. The keynote of all the prayers in these meetings is, 'O Iesu Anwyl!' ('O Precious Jesus'). I have no hesitation in saying that the revival here is decidedly ethical."

THE REV. J. MORGAN,
BRYNSEION C. M. CHURCH, TRECYNON, ABERDARE

"I should like to state that all the denominations have thrown themselves heartily to the movement, and have lost sight entirely of our differences in the one great object of winning souls for Christ.

"The revival has changed the entire character of the town and its surroundings. The churches have been saturated, by the influence of the Holy Spirit. Public houses have been neglected, the football teams have been abandoned, the billiard table has been ignored, gambling given up, foul literature has been done away with, books on hypnotism and skepticism have been burned, foul language we hear none, prayer meetings are held day and night among the colliers of the district."

THE REV. P. CALLIER,
WESLYAN CHURCH, PONTYPRIDD

"Your request is difficult to comply with, except in a very general and imperfect form. I am in the midst of it, in full sympathy with it, and could tell a Scotch or English congregation about it easier than I can write you offhand. The revival surrounds Pontypridd, pervades the atmosphere. Its source is manifestly divine, in the opinion of one who went not to criticize, but receive and help all he could; the effects are such as agree with the character of the Holy Inspirer, and anointed and consecrated human agent. I have no more doubt of its being a work of God than I have of my own existence. As to describing the revival and estimating its results, can you put in words those deep and hallowed experiences of life realized when God meets you almost palpably and sways your whole being crossward, heavenward, and the atmosphere trembles with light, life, love, joy, praise, reverence, awe? (I know some sacred things vouchsafed during this revival.) Did Peter or any of the other apostles express and compress all that was seen and felt on the day of Pentecost? Did Barnabas supply the church at Jerusalem with a report of what he witnessed at Antioch? Who can comprehend the real, outstanding effects presented to the eye of faith, but the One who, in the shadow close at hand, makes His presence felt in, under, behind, and over all the phases of this remarkable movement? You see it is so unique that it is impossible to compare it with past revivals. There are so many new features in the methods, agents, varied manifestations of the Spirit's working, strange and startling phases. No organization whatever, nor arrangement for opening and closing the services. Note the spontaneity, joyousness, freshness, freedom, vocal music consecrated and employed; Celtic temperament mastered and appropriated for a sacred purpose; and the bilingual difficulty no barrier to success. It is glorious. I can imagine if John Wesley and Howell Harris wanted a holiday outside heaven they would spend it in South Wales. The results are so varied in kind and manifold in character that the bare numerical returns afford no criterion whatever, either of the depth, genuineness, or extent of the work. Its ramifications materially affect family, social, commercial, industrial, educational, and church life, and all classes of the community feel its influence. All the churches are quickened as never before, and the ministers of all denominations, Welsh and English, seem to have forgotten their differences of creed and church polity. `Judah does not vex Ephraim,' etc. Wait until the various churches of the next generation are staffed and equipped for home and foreign service, then, in your old age, call a convention for testimony. It will be a revelation! Excuse more; the subject is too big and still growing, to be dealt with in a brief paragraph. Let me close by saying you have made a mistake—have applied to the wrong persons. The ministers are too favorably impressed to form an unbiased judicial opinion."

THE REVIVAL IN WALES: REVIVAL SPIRIT SPREADING IN ENGLAND

All over England a new spirit of prayerfulness and expectation has been awakened in connection with what we call our "ordinary services," and ministers and people now are beginning to realize that it is gloriously possible to have an outpouring of the Holy Spirit without the presence of a special missioner. And when once this conviction gets a firm grip of the imagination and heart of the people, the revival will soon follow.

Statistics give but a very faint idea of the growth and prevalence of this revival, and yet a few figures taken at random show how the flame is spreading. At Dowlais there were 1,000 inquirers before Evan Roberts arrived; at Ebbw Vale they have had 1,500; Risca and Cross Keys, 1,250; East Glamorgan Baptist churches report 7,250, of whom 6,500 are expected to become members; the Rhondda Baptist churches alone have 3,000 new members;

Tredegar, regarded as about the most difficult soil for evangelism, is rejoicing over 1,400 inquirers, 300 of whom came to Christ during the four days visit of Sydney Evans and his helpers.

And so we might go on, for it is believed that the numbers now in North and South Wales do not fall short of 70,000. Drunkenness is still on the decrease. Superintendent Cole, at Pontypridd, reports a gradual decrease in the number of police court cases, and a distinct improvement in the morals of the district. Last Saturday not one case of drunkenness was reported at the police court from Llynfi Valley (20,000 inhabitants), only one, from Garw Valley, and none from Bridgend, Ogmore Valley, and Porthcawl; so the court at Bridgend was able to rise (adjourn. Ed.) at 12:45, some hours earlier than usual. On a recent day at Newport there were only two cases before the court, and this so soon after the white gloves' sitting; and throughout Monmouthshire there is a marked diminution in drunkenness, whilst in many localities swearing, once so common, has altogether ceased.

At the recent International Rugby football match at Cardiff, when 40,000 people were present, a Baptist minister From Bristol told me that he only heard one oath, and he at once reproved the offender, who thanked him for the rebukes shook hands, and said it should not occur again. This was an hour before the match began, and the conversation attracted much interest. As soon as the incident passed over some one who witnessed it struck up *Throw Out the Life Line*, and the chorus was instantly caught up by 10,000 voices. This alone speaks volumes!

The Welsh are supposed to be a Bible-reading people, and judging by the numerous and apt quotations in their prayers they know a great deal more about the contents of the Book than the average man to whom we are accustomed to listen in our English prayer meetings. And yet again and again when Evan Roberts has tested the congregations it has been found that even among Christian people Bible readers are in a minority. Those who have confessed their neglect have promised to amend their ways, and they have so far kept their vow by purchasing Bibles in large quantities. The increase in the sales has been very great. A bookseller at Ton, in the heart of the Rhondda, who has been eighteen years in the trade, says the increase has been most marked "tremendous" is her word for it—and there has been a corresponding decrease in the sale of low-class literature.

So say two booksellers in the neighboring town of Pentre, who add that the most remarkable increase has been in the purchase of pocket Testaments by young men. At Neath a bookseller states that before the revival he regarded Bibles as dead stock but in recent weeks he had cleared out all his old stock and has had to get further supplies. To some of his customers the Bible was quite unknown, and they carried it off as hoarded treasure. Along with this there has been a decided slump in penny dreadfuls.

Good news comes from the Garw Valley, from the Rhondda and elsewhere to the effect that the churches are realizing the importance of providing suitable accommodation for social clubs under

Christian management. The peril of backsliding is very great if no provision is made for enabling young workingmen to spend their leisure hours sensibly, and under conditions that are healthy for their morals. The need of institutional churches in these densely populated districts is recognized, especially considering the large number of public houses and drinking clubs. It is certain that these "houses of Satan" will make a determined effort to win back their former patrons as soon as the first glow of the revival is over. One notable convert who had a very lucrative commission agency in the sporting world, which he instantly abandoned on his conversion, has spoken out very forcibly on this question, and it is satisfactory to find that it is being discussed thoroughly in the local papers.

A young collier, just up from the pit, told me the now familiar tale of the effects of the revival on a large proportion of the 1,100 men who work in his pit. He told me, too, of one public house that formerly sold five barrels of beer in the week, but has only sold half a barrel in the last six weeks, and as a consequence has changed hands. This was confirmed the next day by a young solicitor whose mother most hospitably entertained me, and who had traveled the previous day with a wealthy brewer. A month ago he was laughing heartily at the revival, but now he and the owners of two other breweries in the neighborhood are finding out that when public houses cease to consume, they cease to give orders, and all three now admit that the last month has been the worst for the trade they have known. One of these firms that formerly had to borrow horses to keep pace with the heavy demand on barrels, has not only ceased to borrow, but has been compelled to part with three of its own horses that were out of work, but were feeding heavily.

Many English people may not know that the Welsh collier always speaks of his comrades who work along with him in his own section in the pit as his "butties"—"pals" is the English equivalent perhaps in the vernacular of the street. "Butties" are very loyal to one another, and if one of their number is in trouble, or is being bullied by others, his "butties" always rally to his aid. I make this statement as introductory to one of the most pathetic interruptions of which I have yet heard in a revival service. A minister was dwelling very vividly on the Savior's sufferings, and picturing the scene between Gethsemane and Calvary, when they scoffed at Him and spat upon Him. A young collier was so moved by the story that he sprang to his feet and exclaimed passionately, "Oh, where were His butties?" Such was this rough pitman's commentary on Matt. 26:56, "Then all the disciples left Him and fled."

London Methodist Times

THE STORY OF EVAN ROBERTS' EARLY LIFE

"The child is father of the man" (Wordsworth).

"It is good that a man should both hope and quietly wait for the salvation of the Lord. It is good for a man that he should bear the yoke in his youth" (Lamentations 3:26, 27).

"A servant of Jesus Christ, called. . . separated unto the gospel of God" (Romans 1:1).

Evan Roberts is the son of godly parents. His mother desired that, if it were the will of God, one of her sons should be a preacher. And when Evan was born she said, "I have another son to serve God now; and perhaps he may one day be a preacher."

The Roberts' Home Loughor

Hannah Roberts

Henry Roberts

He was born at Loughor, a village eight miles from Swansea; and in his case, as also at the birth of six other sons and three daughters, prayers and hymns of thanksgiving were heard in the happy cottage home. He received his share, and no more than his share, of his mother's care and love. They were all trained in the nurture and admonition of the Lord.

USEFUL AND OBEDIENT

Evan was always an obedient child, honoring his father and mother; attentive to his teachers at school as one who had been a schoolmate said, "However difficult the lesson, Evan knew it." He was fond of play, like other boys; brave withal, and ready to defend the weaker ones from any youthful tyrants who would take advantage of them.

As he grew, he found many ways of being useful to his mother; when he was twelve years old his father's foot was hurt by an accident in the mine, but as soon as the injury permitted of his return to work, Evan begged to be allowed to go also. Thus it was found that he could be helpful to his father, who held a responsible position, and could not be spared longer than was absolutely necessary. Describing the position at this time of the future evangelist, a contemporary says, "So Evan Roberts, the little Welsh boy of twelve, laid aside his childhood. Almost literally he became his father's right hand, until Mr. Robert recovered from his accident, Evan began to know the hard, perilous life of the miner, for, after some months under his father, he commenced regular work as a mine boy.

"It was at this time apparently that his thoughts began to turn to religion. He did his work underground at the colliery cheerfully and well, and soon was put on to the ordinary shifts.

STUDIOUS AND RELIGIOUS

"'No,' his father told a man at work in the same stall with him, 'the lad belongs to no choir or club. He just goes home and works at his books. It's hard to get him to bed before three or four in the morning.'

"One day came his first opportunity for doing active religious work. The Wesleyan Chapel at Gorscinon did not include in the Sunday school a miners' children's class. Evan Roberts set to work to form such a class. He went to Mr. Thomas, the manager of the mine, and asked if he might use the mine offices on a Sunday.

"'What for?' asked the manager.

"'For a Sunday-school,' was the reply.

"The offices were lent, and the class started. Evan became secretary, and threw his whole soul into the work. Within a few weeks, the 'mine school' was known throughout the district. Many of the children were ragged and shoeless. Evan gave himself and induced some of his friends to help. Presently the minister of the chapel was willing to include the mine children in the ordinary Sunday school.

"The mine work continued, but ever before this boy, now growing into young manhood, was the one object. He would be a preacher. The religion of the home was his, that deep, abiding reverence and fear of God which is frequently met with in cottage homes of the Welsh miners. But as yet that mysterious awakening, that strange call to the service of God, had not come.

"He and his brother Dan played and sang together on the organ in the trim little house overlook-
ing the bleak Llangannack Hills. On Sunday evenings the family gathered together in those reverent, informal home services.

Dan Roberts

Loved Bible Study

As to a subject of study, he seems to have been
devoted to the Word of God.

"The Bible was almost the entire study of Evan
Roberts in these days. He was never seen without a
Testament near him. It was a familiar sight in the
Mountain Colliery to see him going down in the
cage with his Bible in his hand. During the intervals
of work, he studied by the light of his Davy lamp [This
is a typical Welsh miner's lamp. It was designed by
Sir Humphrey Davy and had no naked flame to
ignite methane gas in the mines. Ed.]. He was just
preparing for the future, and there was no attempt
at preaching or anything but study at this time.

"'I will be a preacher,' he said definitely, and was willing to work and wait for the appointed time. The money he earned some 30S. or £2 a week after he had contributed his share towards the home, he saved or expended on books. It was a strange life. For eight hours out of twenty-four he was miner, giving all his physical energies to the work; for the remaining sixteen he was an earnest young student, slowly climbing into the heights of religious thought. So the boy grew almost to manhood."

But Evan never liked a miner's life, though he worked conscientiously and well. Every spare minute, out came his New Testament, and standing or sitting on a piece of coal he would forget everything else.

When he was nearly twenty, he began to think of further education. A deacon gave him a list of books to read, in addition to his Bible, which was always his chief study. He also thought shorthand would be of use to him. Accordingly Evan found a friend living three miles off who could teach him, and for three months he walked the six miles until he knew shorthand. He neglected none of his work in the mine, and was reading books which required close thought.

He had an uncle to whom he now bound himself to learn the blacksmith's trade, insisting on paying £6 of money which he had saved. In a few months he became a capable worker, and valuable to his uncle.

Then came the beginning of his career as a preacher. He had been asked to preach at one of the chapels, but had refused, for he had not yet received the call from above. An earnest young deacon preached one night, and said that if any one desired the Spirit of God for service, He would come by constant and unwearying prayer. Evan went home and prayed long and earnestly, and towards morning rose from his knees with his mind fully made up to go to the Ministers' Training College at Newcastle Emlyn. His mother was overjoyed. The desire and prayer of her life was about to be fulfilled. The family contributed to the fees, which were lightened by his assisting in some of the minor duties of the college.

After he had been there about a year, he received the wonderful call which has resulted in the present revival.

With the great movement which grew out of those first meetings at Loughor our readers are familiar. The long-prayed-for revival is with us, and there will assuredly be much prayer, and fervent, that its gracious power may not only spread throughout the length and breadth of our own loved land, but that all nations may come to feel the hallowed influence of these "breezes from Calvary's hill."

M. . .
London Christian

REVIVAL SPREADS IN ALL DIRECTIONS

When Mr. Evan Roberts visited Resolven last week, all the neighboring collieries were idle, and from the outlying hamlets people crowded into the pretty Neath Valley township. Mountain and valley lay covered with snow, the white mantel prompting an ardent Welshman to exclaim, "Wales is physically white now; she is going to be morally and spiritually white." The revival fire has burned brightly at Resolven, and 600 converts are reported. Last week an impressive revival service (promoted by all the Resolven churches, Established and Free), was held at St. David's (parish) church. The vicar, Rev. William Lloyd, was unable to attend, owing to ill health, but the meeting was most fervent, and was conducted entirely on revival lines.

AT HIRWAIN

The two-days' mission conducted by Mr. Evan Roberts at Hirwain attracted a stream of visitors from London and other parts of the United Kingdom. Among those who took part in the meetings were a number of converted Jews. On the second afternoon, the missioner attended Nebo Welsh Congregational Church. *Gawn ni gwrdd tu draw i'r Afon*, was sung with great fervor, and was repeated again and again. When some of the singers seemed inclined to stop, Mr. Roberts remarked, "Go on singing, it is blessed to be here."

The missioner again emphasized the duty of complete submission to the commands of the Spirit. He urged all to bend. Would they not rather bend under the tender hand of God's love than to be bent by His anger? An appeal to the missioner on behalf of the English friends present for a few words in English was met with the prompt reply, "I will be guided by the Spirit. I will speak in English immediately the Spirit commands me to do so."

He referred in tremulous tones to a wonderful experience on the previous evening. This led him to deal with the ministry of suffering. Hymns and prayers followed, a feature of the prayers being the appeals of mothers for the conversion of prodigal and impenitent sons. The missioner read from the Book of Joel, then appealed for confessions. A few commenced here and there to testify of their love for Christ, and were soon joined by a great host, the scene being indescribable.

Many rushed from the afternoon meeting to Bethel Chapel in hope of hearing Evan Roberts in the evening, but even then the chapel was crowded. So dense was the throng that a constable had to assist the missioner in gaining admission. The chapel has seating accommodation for 900 people, but there were about 2,000 packed in the building. There were again many stirring scenes and confessions of Christ.

AT DOWLAIS

At Dowlais, on Sunday last, the morning service was held at Elizabeth Street English Methodist Church, and fully an hour before the missioner made his appearance the building was taxed to its utmost capacity. The congregation included visitors from various parts of the kingdom, among them Lady Wimborne.

Mr. Roberts spoke for some time in English, and his words made a deep impression. The meeting was pervaded with a feeling of solemn reverence. The missioner dwelt feelingly on the necessity of a public declaration, and appealed to the congregation not to be afraid to express their thoughts, either by singing or praying. "Let us," he said, "pray to become full of faith for Christ."

A young man in the gallery started a pathetic (passionate. Ed.) Welsh hymn, and it was sung with inspiring effect. A fervent prayer from the same quarter followed, and a young woman, whose voice was choked with sobs, rose and prayed softly in Welsh. "Come to save, Lord!" was the burden of her cry, and she sat down, overcome by her feelings. Hymn after hymn followed, English and Welsh commingling (both languages blended into a harmonious whole. ed.).

The meeting in the afternoon was somewhat "hard," and Mr. Roberts was deeply pained. The evening meeting was held at Hermon Congregational Chapel, and the crush here was tremendous. Police officers helped at guarding the entrance to the chapel, and the gates had to be locked long before the time of meeting. Notwithstanding this, however, a huge crowd congregated outside the chapel, and carried on a service of their own. Inside the building there was a lack of fire, which moved the missioner to ask for greater fervor, and this had the desired effect for a time. The meeting, however, again grew cold, and Mr. Roberts brought it to a conclusion.

AT PENTIR

With the Bishop of Bangor's sanction, an eight days' mission—January 15-22—was held in the parish of Pentir, near Bangor. The parochial missioner was Rev. James Davies, St. David's, Liverpool. The mission commenced by the Dean of Bangor preaching a mission sermon, and giving an address at the after-meeting. The work of the mission had a powerful effect upon the parishioners. Many joined the church, thus renewing the life and adding to the strength of the church in this slate-quarry district. A good and solid preparation had been made by the vicar, Rev. Herbert Jones, assisted by Rev. John Pryce-Jones, curate. To every appearance the result of the mission will be more vigor in church work and a marked increase in the congregation.

AT BANGOR

In the course of a smoke room conversation at Bangor University College last week, among half a dozen of the students, one of them touched on the subject of the revival expressing the opinion that it was a real thing. A second student thereupon started a hymn tune, another prayed, and ere long hymns and prayers were in full swing. The singing attracted other students, and presently the smoke room was crowded to its utmost capacity. The students "cut" lectures, and remained in this impromptu prayer meeting from 11 to 1:30. In the afternoon from 300 to 400 of the students attended a prayer meeting at one of the chapel school rooms at which five lady students in turn engaged in prayer. At night the students formed a procession and marched, singing through the streets to the tabernacle, the largest chapel in the town, which was soon filled with a fervent crowd of worshipers. The interest of the students is remarkable, as hitherto they have, as a body, manifested no particular interest in the revival.

THE REVIVAL OF BIBLE STUDY

A meeting of the Ebbw Vale auxiliary of the Bible Society partook largely of the character of a revival meeting. Dr. Cynddylan Jones said Wales had a revival 150 years ago, when the inhabitants flocked to hear Daniel Rowlands, who was afterwards known by the nickname of the "cracked clergyman of Llangeitho." In 1859-60 they had another revival, and now they were experiencing another. During the last three months there had been a great moving of the people. Who among them anticipated the country would be shaken by a boy from school?

The revival would be judged by results. From the chief depot of the Bible Society, during November and December, £300 worth of Bibles had been sent to Wales and Monmouthshire, as compared with £80 for the two preceding months. This was evidence that the revival was not emotionalism. No revival would last without the Bible. After Dr. Jones had concluded, there was prayer and praise, and a number of seekers were pointed to Christ.

In an earnest address on mission work, given by Dr. Henry Soltau at a drawing room meeting at the residence of Mr. W. H. Vellacott, West Thurrock, Essex, the speaker alluded to a recent visit by some of his friends to the Welsh revival districts. First of all, they went to the locality where Mr. Evan Roberts was present. The Spirit of God was manifest in a marked degree. Then, traveling many miles away, where Mr. Roberts had not been, they found similar deeply spiritual manifestations. Unable to get lodgings at a private house, they reluctantly took up their abode at a hotel, where drinking was going on in a bar at the front of the house. "We had better stay," said one of the visitors, "perhaps God has sent us here." The chapels in the district were densely crowded, and the meetings prolonged to a very late hour. It was past midnight before the party returned to the hotel.

About two o'clock in the morning one of the visitors was aroused from his sleep with a message that the landlord urgently desired to see him. The proprietor of the hotel was in his room in deep agony of mind, and exclamations such as, "Oh, I'm a great sinner," "Tell me how I can be saved," came from his lips.

"If you are in earnest," replied the evangelist, "you will cry to God." The man did so; and while the Gospel was being simply and lovingly spoken, he rose from his knees and declared that, great sinner as he had been ("I've been on the drink," he added, "for weeks.") he knew he had now received the Lord Jesus as his Savior. The next day he made an open confession of Christ, and two men in his employment, who had also been great drunkards, went down on their knees confessing their sins, and professed to find the Lord.

AT LLANFAIR-CAEREINION

The Free Churches of Llanfair-Caereinion have started aggressive work with earnestness. Crowded prayer meetings resolve themselves into musical processions along the main streets, and some local publicans are already beginning to complain. The landlord of one hotel recently said he had lost £35 in a few weeks. Some retaliatory measures were adopted. One night 150 men and women assembled on Llanfair Square. The procession marched past the hotel, opposite which a young lady started *Bydd canu yn y nefoedd* (*There Will Be Song in Heaven*). On the return journey, made in some places through snow six inches deep, the crowd stopped near the hotel, singing *Diolch Iddo* (*Thanks Be to Him*). As soon as the hymn was finished, the street was filled with the sound of dance music, emitted from a powerful gramophone placed in the front window. The sound was immediately drowned in a volume of *Yn ydyfroedd mawr a'r tonau* (*In the Waves and Mighty Waters*), and the singers resumed their way.

AT MOLD AND LLANFAIRFECHAN

The revival continues to gather force in North Wales. A meeting held at Mold was remarkable for its power and effect. The leader was Rev. Seth Joshua (who was used of God in leading Evan Roberts into a glorious experience). Mr. Joshua called upon all the men present to sing a verse of *I Surrender*, and urged them to let the surrender include football, billiards, drink, and everything that kept them from Jesus Christ. Then he called upon the women to sing a verse, and asked them to let the surrender include attendance at dances, chitchat, gossip, and backbiting, all expensive forms of dress and living, and whatever hindered their progress as Christians. At the close of the meeting a large number of converts came forward. Prayer meetings are being held in all Nonconformist places of worship at Mold. It has now been ascertained that the number of conversions, as a direct result of the revival movement in the Nantile Vale district alone, reaches the total of 480.

Rev. T. C. Roberts, Llanfairfechan, says, "The revival was first felt in Llanfairfechan during the last week in November. The following week all the chapels had special prayer meetings, which were well attended, and were the means of arousing the whole place. Hardly a night passed in any of the chapels without some converts. The following week we had united prayer meetings and special services. The week after all the chapels had their own meetings. Every Saturday evening from the commencement we have had a united prayer meeting, either in one of the largest chapels or in the Public Hall, and, wherever it is held, the place is always packed. Every Saturday evening, previous to the meeting, there is always a procession through the whole place. The women also are having a united prayer meeting twice a week, which is well attended, and a great means of blessing. The workmen also are having prayer meetings in the Penmaur Quarries at the dinner hour. Since the revival came there is a vast improvement in the moral tone and behavior of the whole place."

AT MENAI BRIDGE

Rev. T. Charles Williams, Menai Bridge, says, "The meetings are characterized by much spiritual fervor, and many dozens have taken part in public worship for the first time. There are over sixty converts. The prayers of the children in some of the meetings have been remarkable in their effect. The revival broke out in this place without any visible human agency, and the movement is not directly guided by anyone. The ministers have thrown themselves heart and soul into it. Prayer meetings are to be held every evening this week, and the Welsh Methodist Chapel, the largest building in the place, has on more than one occasion proved too small. The force and reality of the movement here is not challenged by anyone, and there can be no doubt that its effect will be lasting and beneficial."

AT RISCA, FLEUR-DE-LIS, AND LLANGEFUI

The movement is making great progress at Risca and district, and many conversions are reported: Bethany (Baptist), 130; Glyn (Congregational), 150; Primitive Methodist, 15; Wesleyan, 14; Moriah (Baptist), 300. At Cross Keys: Hope (Baptist), 165; Trinity (Congregational), 280; Primitive Methodist, 130; Wesleyan, 40.

A pathetic scene that brought tears to the eyes of many who witnessed it took place at New Salem Chapel, Fleur-de-Lis. Among the converts was an old man who went to kneel at the penitent form. He was almost immediately joined by his crippled daughter, who had to come up the chapel on crutches. The silence, for a moment, was most impressive, and then the singing of *Diolch Iddo* seemed to shake the very building.

A party of half a dozen Bangor Baptist and other students visited Llangefui on Thursday last. It was market day. They started a prayer meeting in the center of the crowded market, and the marketing was instantly abandoned, the people enthusiastically joining in the religious service. Mr. William Jones, M. P., associated himself with the proceedings.

London Christian

AN INCIDENT OF THE REVIVAL

I must give yet another splendid story of a different type of man which my kind friend, the C. M. (Calvinistic Methodist. Ed.) pastor of Brynseion, narrated to me in our long and pleasant interview last Saturday morning.

It is the case of David Jones, a man of fifty-eight, and a noted character in that locality. He has long been a comic singer, a man of fluent speech and ready wit. As a comedian he was the center of attraction wherever he went. It paid any publican to give him drink. He could always pack any public house, and make the trade hum.

One day at the end of November, after the revival had been in progress about a fortnight, a publican met this man's daughter, a fine girl of eighteen, and said, "Miss Jones, where is your father? Is he from home? Is he unwell? I haven't seen him for a fortnight." She said, "He's not from home, and he is not unwell, but he is very comfortable on his own hearth, and you are not likely to see him again."

"What's the matter?" he asked. "Has this silliness taken hold of him?" "Silliness! What do you mean?" "Why, the revival, of course." "Oh, if that's the silliness, then I am in the midst of it, and my father is on the eve of being captivated by it as well." He scoffed at her, and said, "I'll take good care to have my bird in hand again in less than a week. I can't afford to lose your father, and won't."

"Do you mean to say that you are going to influence him to come back to the drink when he is doing his utmost to resist it?" "Oh, yes, I do," he said. She stamped her little foot vigorously, and said, "Well, it will be a terrible struggle between Jesus, my Savior, and Satan; and I warn you of this, Jesus has not yet lost one battle with Satan, and He won't."

A week later, however, she came to the service, and bursting into tears said to the people, "I'm sorry to say the publican has verified his statement and got my father back, and on Saturday night he came home again under the influence of the cup. But I am satisfied he has come home for the last time in that state. Are you willing for Satan and the publican to have my father? Isn't it right for Jesus, who has suffered and died for him, to have him? I am now going to pray God to save him this very moment, and I want you to pray silently with me." It was a most moving speech, and then she prayed like an angel—a prayer that was more moving still. Everybody said that prayer must have gone straight to the throne and to the Father's heart.

The people remained some time in silent prayer. Mrs. Morgan's (the minister's wife) faith was great, and she said to her husband, "Go out and see if David Jones is lurking around the chapel, and bring him in." He smiled at her doubtingly, and she said, "Why do you not believe? God will certainly answer prayer."

He went out at her request, but David Jones was not to be seen. When the service closed at 11:15, Mr. Morgan went with his wife and daughter to his house. The comic singer had gone to bed. One of his daughters went upstairs, and he called out gruffly, "Who's there?" "Rev. John Morgan, of Brynseion, Father." "What does he want here at this time of night?" he asked in a voice that could be distinctly heard below. "He wants to see you, I expect."

"Please tell his reverence that he won't see me tonight, and say that if Edward VII, king of England, asked me to come down tonight, that I would refuse."

As soon as Miss Morgan, the minister's daughter, that sweet girl of fifteen to whom I formerly alluded, heard those words, she jumped up, fell on her knees, and clutching her father's knees as he sat still, prayed with such anguish of spirit for this man that both families were melted into tears. It seemed as if such a prayer must be irresistible. I saw that young girl last week. She is tall, thin, pale, and with refined features, and a very peaceful expression, like her mother. Then Mrs. Morgan prayed fervently, and then her husband knelt at the foot of the stairs, and prayed up the stairs, and higher up still! When he finished, His daughter came and knelt beside him, and sang up the stairs, "For you I am praying."

They all thought that David Jones must now relent, and they waited and waited prayerfully in a silence that was awful, but no! There was not a sound, not a stir, nor a sign of any description.

When the minister rose to leave, he took good care to say to the man's wife and daughter, "Now, do be as kind and tenderhearted as possible to him tomorrow, and don't reproach him in the least. And don't say another word to him about it tonight." They did as he advised. Next morning his daughter prepared his breakfast as usual, but not a word was mentioned about the midnight prayer meeting. He went out quietly, and came back at night in good time, and still not a word of reference.

Just the same again on Friday morning, but when he returned in the evening and had washed and had tea, he thought fit to break the seal of silence himself, and said to his daughter, who was to him a real ministering angel, "Now, dear, bring the Bible to the table and read a chapter to your father for the first time." She did so, and then added, confidently, "And now, father, shall I pray?" "No, no; you sha'n't pray with me. You leave it between me and my God, and go to the meeting."

"Very well, father, I will do as you wish, but promise me one thing—you will come yourself tomorrow night."

He said he would, and true to his word, he turned up at the united open-air demonstration, which has been quite a feature on Saturday evenings of this revival movement. The minister's daughter soon spied him out, and said to her father, "Do go at once and grip his hand, and let him know your heart is very warm, and how glad we shall all be to see him at chapel."

He came as he said he would, but neither on Saturday nor Sunday would he yield. He was so deliberate about it all that some began to lose faith, but those who knew the man knew well how terribly he realized the responsibility of his position, and how his heart yearned for rest. On Monday there was another private conference between him and Mr. Morgan, which ended in his decision to be present that night in good time in order to secure a good seat.

From the start the service seemed to be quite independent of human control, and the sense of the Divine Presence was very real to them all. At nine o'clock, when the house was being "tested," and one decision after another was being announced, in each case accompanied by *Diolch Iddo*, the song of the new birth, David Jones retained his seat, looking very serious and anxious, whilst it was evident to all he was being torn with conflicting emotions. In that joyous crowd he seemed to be almost the only one who knew no joy, and this emphasized his sense of loneliness in his awful fight with his stern foe.

Mr. Morgan at last resorted to a plan which helped the faith of all, and especially that of the unhappy comedian.

"Have we not all been praying?" *En masse* the people shouted, "Yes." "For whom have we all been praying?" Instantly, they thundered back, "For David Jones." "Can not God save him now, and will He not?" With one voice they replied, "Yes."

This gave the finishing touch, and broke clean asunder the chains that had so long held the poor man in the bondage of Satan. He was completely "bent," and then he was blessedly saved. Ecstasy seems but a poor word with which to describe the transports of joy into which the huge congregation plunged straight away, and it was a long time before their tears were dried and their voices were hushed. To this day David Jones' salvation is regarded as a direct answer to the prayers of the church. They were violent, and they took the kingdom of heaven by force.

Rev. T. Ferrier Htclme
London Methodist Times

THE WELSH REVIVAL

We have reports of a wonderful religious awakening which is taking place in Wales. The work seems to be wrought by the Holy Spirit through Christians who are wholly given up to God for use rather than by organization and program, which so often characterize modern revivals. This revival is the result of prayer and humble dependence upon God.

The result is that it is the most remarkable religious upheaval that has taken place since 1859-60. Places of amusement have been abandoned in many towns, and the people have thronged these evangelistic meetings and found Christ precious as the sinner's friend. There is mighty conviction upon the people, and it is said that some 10,000 have recently professed Christ. The following report is given of one of these meetings:

"Mr. Sidney Evans was the central figure at a wonderful meeting held at Trinity Chapel, Lianelly. The building was packed at seven o'clock, and the proceedings were protracted until two o'clock on the following morning.

Sidney Evans

"The tide of feeling was high, when a young man rose in the gallery and asked the congregation to join him in prayer on behalf of his wayward brother; there was a remarkable outburst. This was accentuated when a well-known workingman walked into the penitents' pew, fell on his knees in a paroxysm (spasm, outbreak. Ed.) of weeping, and sobbed a broken prayer for forgiveness. In his moment of self-abandonment, he described how, like the prodigal son, he had gone to a far country, but was recalled to his better self by prayer meetings held at the works. His story moved all who heard it, and there was not a dry eye in the chapel as the pathetic (emotional. Ed.) recital went on. Many penitents were pointed to Christ.

"Shortly before 11 o'clock it was decided to make a tour of the New Dock district, and hundreds of people formed themselves into a procession. They marched through the streets singing hymns, and gathering strength as they went along. A number of men and women under the influence of drink were approached, and all these were persuaded to return to the chapel, where prayer was offered on their behalf. The converts included sailors, tin-plate workers, colliers, and several women, all falling on their knees and asking for forgiveness. Mr. Evans and others prayed with them, and this went on until the Sabbath had been ushered in.

Would to God that the fire would spread, and that this needy land might be reached by a wave of salvation that has never yet been experienced. Let us pray for such an event. God is willing when His people will meet Bible conditions. May God, awaken a sleeping and slumbering church to a sense of their duty and privilege in these last days. God will hold His people responsible for the best that His Spirit can accomplish through them.

Gospel Message

THE GREAT REVIVAL IN WALES
H. S. HALLMAN

Mrs. Penn-Lewis writes in *Life of Faith* that the work of the Spirit is showing not the least sign of abatement; that the Christmas holidays had no effect on it as far as killing or checking this great movement. Like a great wave it sweeps over the land, submerging everything within its reach. Evan Roberts, though still a leading man wherever he appears, yet he is comparatively a small "incident" in relation to the whole movement. The revival is no respecter of persons, and denominationalism does not count.

Describing a meeting at Ebenezer Chapel, Swansea, she says, "The chapel was crowded, with hundreds in the street, an hour before the meeting was timed to begin. The aisles were packed; the window ledges filled; the occupants of the 'set fawr' tightly wedged therein. There is neither orator nor singer to touch the people, and yet they are moved by an unseen power. Prayers and singing follow one another, and a young girl stands and recites in Welsh, with her face aglow with joy, the parable of the Prodigal Son. It is said that the packed audience listened as to a new-found tale, and when the story reached the point of the father running to greet the lost one, it burst out into a rousing rendering of the hymn *Diolch Iddo*! *(Praise Him*!)

"Mr. Evan Roberts' theme was giving to God. They could not compete with God in giving! He gave His Son, His greatest gift. He was the 'Way' to everything, except destruction. Men might keep their scraps. God needed none of them. The audience broke into tears, for the missioner found himself describing Gethsemane, and emotion choked his utterances. Tear-stained faces were seen on every side, and then a young lady described her conversion, and recited the Welsh hymn, *O That I Could Love the Lord more Faithfully!* The people rose *en masse,* and sang it again and again. The Vicar of Swansea leads in prayer, and the missioner proceeds again, describing now dark Calvary. A woman breaks out amid sobs into the Welsh hymn, 'And was it for my sins that my Lord was crucified?' 'And of His own will was He nailed to the tree,' adds another. The congregation then softly sang in subdued tones these hymns, whilst others offered prayer.

"'My mission is first to the churches,' the missioner afterwards said. When the churches are aroused to their duty, men of the world will be swept into the kingdom. A whole church on its knees is irresistible! 'How many of you have received the baptism of the Spirit?' he asked the congregation. Will any respond? Yes, quite a dozen are on their feet; and a voice comes from somewhere in the gallery, 'For thirty-eight years a member of a Christian church, but it is not until this afternoon that I received the baptism of the Spirit.'

"Surely this is Pentecost! It is not only an awakening of sinners, but the church being brought back by God Himself to her primitive and rightful condition.

"God is working in mighty power in other places. At Ystradgynlais at one meeting, the building, holding 1,500 people, was packed. Many people sobbed, and even the strongest men were unable to restrain their tears. A minister prayed with great

intensity, and then referred to past differences between himself and two other ministers. They had
written against one another in the papers, but now
they were going to shake hands to the glory of God.
The three ministers were now in the pulpit, and shook
hands before the people. It is said that the joy that
prevailed baffled description, and converts came
forward by the dozen. Converts by the dozen will
come forward in England when they see the children of God acting like this. Oh, Spirit of melting—
come upon us!

"At Hengoed, in an evening service, the pastor
gave an opportunity to those who had quarreled,
or were in disagreement, to heal the breach, and
an old man, laboring under deep emotion, left the
gallery, and entering a seat on the ground floor,
extended his hand to another. They were father and
son.

"In Cwmavon during a three days' mission,
when the Spirit of God wrought mightily, during one
of the meetings a young man in a state of great
agitation, and with tears streaming down his face,
made his way to one of the pews, and to another
young man held out his hands, and in a voice
choked with emotion said, 'Forgive me.' They were
old friends who had become bitter enemies. At first
the appeal was not responded to. The congregation prayed whilst the two retired to the vestry, and
shortly afterwards they were seen praying together,
clasped in each other's arms—reconciled.

"The practical effects of the Holy Spirit's work
compel the attention and respect of many who
would turn aside from the movement on account
of its emotional aspect. The world wants something

'practical,' and asks for visible evidences. Today it has them. In the Rhondda Valley, at a service, a pastor calls attention to the habit of people making purchases late on Saturday nights, thus keeping shopkeepers and assistants at work till past midnight, and grocery carts delivering goods till the early hours of Sunday. The people are willing now to listen to the claims of their fellowmen, and all present quickly bind themselves to shop before nine o'clock on Saturday nights.

"We have already referred to the effect of the revival in the colleges of Wales. Professor Ellis Edwards, of Bala, says, concerning the students in Bala College, that if ever he had seen the subduing, melting, abasing, elevating effects of divine power he saw them now. He speaks of the humility, love, and affection, tenderness and desire to help others, witnessed among his students, and tells how, after but a few prayer meetings, there came confession of defects and sins, and men became like children in appeals for God to help, seeking with confidence a sight of Christ.

"The students have carried the blessing with them to their homes. A minister writes of one young lady student being used to start the revival in a chapel which was one of the stiffest to move, and of others stirring up churches in other districts."

It is said that at the close of one meeting—crowded, and gathered only by announcement at an open-air service which preceded it—the effect of the prayers and streams of tears on the faces of the young people made them appear transfigured.

"At an ordinary evening service on New Year's day, in one church, after waiting on the Lord for an hour, a mighty spirit of prayer fell upon the congregation, and every one present, from the child of eleven to the aged man and woman, prayed audibly. All the chapels are continuing nightly prayer meetings.

"The pastor of one church, with a band of ten of his young workers, visited Llanddowror, the birthplace of the famous Griffith Jones, and held a few meetings there, which were crowded, and characterized by deep fervor of prayer. A Carmarthen paper, describing the meetings, says that Rev. M. H. Jones spoke on three stages to be emphasized in such a meeting: (1) Decision for Christ; (2) Surrender to Christ as King; (3) Power for service by the reception of the Holy Spirit. The Spirit of God so completely overpowered the meeting that, long before the close, there was not one left who had not taken some step forward in their inner life. Testimonies followed, and there was ample proof that many had received the Holy Spirit for service, for they were given an eloquence of speech and boldness which made all marvel.

"A private letter from a Londoner who visited the various districts, and was present at a great meeting at Morriston, says that the reports which are given in print fall far short in their effort to convey an account of what is really happening. He had never seen anything approaching this great movement. This seems to be the unvarying testimony of all who 'turn aside to see this great sight' of God breaking forth again as a flame of fire, not in one thorn bush alone, but in thousands of ordinary human beings.

"The following summary of the prominent features of the revival as seen by a minister is given in a private letter:

"1. The spirit of prayer that has fallen upon the people. Prayer meetings are now the most popular of services. Family altars have been erected in scores of homes, and dozens have been started by young people. There are prayer meetings everywhere—in shops, factories, mines, trains, etc.

"2. The rediscovery of the Bible. People read it now for practical purposes. Young Christian workers are anxious to learn how to rightly dispense the truth to needy souls.

"3. Hymns that praise the love of Christ, portray the cross, plead for the Holy Spirit, and aim at saving souls, are the favorites of the people.

"4. The reality and nearness of the great spirit world. Church members now awake to their need of a personal Savior, they come to believe that He can save from the power of sin, and learn to obey the promptings of the Spirit.

"5. Ethical fruits of the revival, viz., reparation, payment of old debts, peacemaking, the giving up of doubtful habits and pleasures, etc.

"In short, the half of what God is working, can never be told by human tongue or pen. Let the story, broken as it is, draw every heart to open to the Spirit of God in the fullness of His power, that He may show also what He can do in England, and in 'all nations.'"

Gospel Banner

THE GREAT WELSH REVIVAL

The great revival in Wales is still spreading. Thousands are being wrought upon by the Spirit in conviction, and thousands are being genuinely converted. The saloons are having to close because there are no customers, and the theaters must shut up because there are no patrons. The following is a description of an "eyewitness," as told in *The Methodist Recorder,* "What we saw on a weekly afternoon in Rhondda Valley, in a chapel which was packed from floor to ceiling, and in which a service of song and testimony had proceeded for two hours before Evan Roberts put in an appearance.

"As he enters, the whole congregation jumps to its feet and jubilantly sings *Diolch Iddo*, etc.:

"'Songs of praises
I will ever give to Thee.'

"This is repeated two or three times over, and then the vast throng settles down to listen.

"He is a young man of some twenty-six summers, who until a few months ago was a working collier. Collier? It seems incredible! Why, look at his radiant face, his refined features, his brilliant, magnetic eyes lit up with a strange and supernal light! Watch the play and movement of his countenance—now smiling, now weeping! Listen to him talking—simply, earnestly, incisively, authoritatively! Withal, how natural, modest, unaffected he is! What is the secret of the spell he wields over that audience? Is it learning or eloquence, or even the proverbial Welsh 'hwyl?' Nothing of the kind. The secret of his power is that he is 'full of faith and love and zeal and the Holy Ghost.' He has been 'baptized,' and is 'possessed.' Of that there can be no doubt. And how anxious he is that all his hearers should enjoy this experience! This is his message that afternoon, and for an hour he is pressing the divine gift of the Spirit upon their acceptance. 'Confess your sins to God,' he pleads with the people; 'Forgive your enemies;' 'Out with every root of bitterness and malice;' 'Bow down your souls at the King's feet;' 'Repent and believe—believe—believe;' 'Trust and obey,' and you shall be 'filled with joy unspeakable and full of glory.' That is the burden of his message. For an hour he pleads with pathos (emotion. Ed.) and passion, and then makes his usual appeal for public confession. The response is immediate and impressive. Moved as if by one mighty impulse, nearly the whole of the congregation is upon its feet, and remains standing for forty minutes, while 'streams of testimony' are issuing forth from men, women, and even children in all parts of the building, hundreds of whom, many for the first time, declare their love for Jesus Christ. It was an extraordinary scene, the like of which I have never before witnessed. Fragments of hymns, verses, and 'experiences,' mingled with sobs and praises, followed each other (sometimes half a dozen at a time in different parts of the chapel) in amazing and Pentecostal profusion, and the missioner frequently clapped his hands for joy! Then an appeal is made to the 'unconverted,' who still remained sitting. 'Who will receive Christ now?' he asks, and instantly there is a chorus of acceptances. As each convert or batch of converts rises, the pent-up people burst again and again into the triumphant strain,

> "'Diolch Iddo,
> Byth am gofio llwch y llawar.'

"It was nearly six o'clock when the meeting closed. Few, however, of those who heard Mr. Roberts that afternoon would hear him again in the evening, for, although announced for seven o'clock at a neighboring chapel, I found that by five o'clock it was crowded to the doors."

MR. ROBERTS DEALING WITH AN INFIDEL

The Rev. D. M. Phillips, of Tylorstown, writing to *The British Weekly* (London) describes a scene in which Evan Roberts himself figured, "The evening service at Ebenezer (Congregational) was a never-to-be-forgotten one. Every corner is filled, and the audience is at least 1,000, and three other chapels are packed at the same time. Now, fancy Evan Roberts, a young man twenty-six years of age, facing this audience! He has only an ordinary education, has not a melodious voice, has but very few strains of oratory, and is far from aiming at creating any sensation. When an ebullition (seething, bubbling. Ed.) of emotion is manifested, he does not take the least advantage of that, and keeps his mental and emotional equilibrium perfectly balanced in the greatest excitement. This meeting, however, is the greatest test on him in the whole series. But he is a complete master of his position. At the end an infidel was discovered in the audience, but he did not wish to own that publicly. This was communicated to the revivalist by a young man who spoke to the infidel in the seat. In an instant Roberts was on his feet, and asked the atheist to stand up to express his unbelief in God's existence.

For some time he refused, but Roberts in a firm manner and in the best feeling insisted that he should. At last he reluctantly got up and said, 'I believe in my heart there is no God.' In a moment a voice from the gallery shouted, 'Out with him,' and there were scores ready to obey the voice; but no sooner had the words dropped from the lips of those in the gallery than the revivalist said in a firm, loving voice, 'No, let us pray for him;' In less than a minute more than thirty were on their knees on behalf of the poor atheist. This was the most dramatic scene that I have ever witnessed in a place of worship. A young man followed the denier of God, and he promised, with tears in his eyes, to take the Bible with him to bed that night to try and get the light. In another ten minutes two other incidents similar to this occurred, with regard to the deity of Christ and the atonement. These were cogently dealt with in less than five minutes by the young revivalist in such a Christian spirit that I shall never forget it. When these oppositions began to pour in, a number of us ministers were trembling, but seeing them disposed of in such a masterly way, we 'praised God, from whom all blessings flow.'"

Here is a beautiful verse from one of the popular songs now being sung by the Welsh people in their marvelous revival meetings:

"Jesus Christ lifts up the weary,
With a smile divinely sweet;
Jesus Christ brings down the mighty,
Kneeling, trembling at His feet
Blessed Savior,
Send *a* breeze from Calvary!"

The Soul Winner

Seventy Thousand Conversions

Welsh Revival Notes

The latest English papers to arrive show that the Welsh revival is deepening and spreading. One of the papers says, "Consensus of opinion among Abertillery tradesmen is that the revival will eventually be good for trade all round. One of the largest drapers in the county said a day or two ago that a man purchased a piece of linoleum and walked out of the shop gladly exclaiming, 'But for the revival I should not have been able to buy this.'"

This interesting story is given by *The Goleuad*, "One of the results of the revival is the action of a South Wales solicitor, who gives up his appointment as legal adviser to the brewers, and thereby sacrifices the sum £12,000 annually." This is $10,000.

In Spurgeon's Tabernacle

The Baptist, London, reports that Mr. Thomas Spurgeon had returned from Wales, and gave an account of the meeting. "Both his sermons on Sunday were devoted to the subject, and he gave the congregation his impressions. There was quite a wave of revivalist enthusiasm in the service at night. Mr. Spurgeon himself, in response to shouts which burst out from many in the congregation early in the sermon, asked the people to rise and, sing the *Doxology*. This they did, and the discourse was then proceeded with. Later some one again interrupted the preacher, this time by starting the singing of *There Is a Fountain Filled with Blood*. The congregations took up the hymn, and then, by no means disconcerted—though he confessed he might not have liked it a week before—Mr. Spurgeon resumed the thread of his remarks at the point previously reached. The text of the sermon was Psalm 118: 23, 'This is the Lord's doings; it is marvelous in our eyes.'"

Evan Roberts, "What have you done for Christ? Have you lost a drop of blood for Him? Have you sweated for Him? Have you given up anything worth mentioning for his sake? You know what he has done for you. Have you, since accepting Christ, done anything to prove it? If you have performed one good action, the world may read a chapter in that single action; for the Bible of the world is the life of the Christian."

A GLIMPSE AT THE MEETING

"At the morning meeting," says the *Western Mail,* "the people were singing when the evangelist stopped them, stating that a man was in distress and was ready to make the 'decision,' and upon this, it was stated that a man had 'given in.' This was the signal as usual for an outburst of *Diolch Iddo,* but they had not sung long before the evangelist stopped the singing, stating that there was another about to 'break through," and he asked where the person indicated was, and then, almost simultaneously, came the reply that another had stood up in the gallery. And subsequently the evangelist stopped the singing several times successively, explaining that there were some in the meeting in great straits and about to make the 'decision,' and 'beseeching the people to pray.' And each time the scenes increased in intensity, and, what is more marvelous, each time there was a convert recorded, as predicted by the missioner. With his face bearing traces of intense emotion, he would announce that someone was in travail of soul. 'It is a hot battle,' he would say, and then exclaim, 'Pray, people, pray; oh, pray, people, pray,' and his request was acceded to on the part of scores of people simultaneously, he himself being engaged in silent prayer. After being thus preoccupied for some time, he would say, 'The decision has been made, and all that is necessary is that he or she should stand up.' Sometimes the announcement of another convert would not be immediately forthcoming, but he would insist that some one had been converted, and ultimately the announcement would be made. So awesome the meeting became that the evangelist said it was now too terrible (fearful, powerful. Ed.) to sing. He had never experienced such a thing before. Someone started very plaintively and prayerfully, *For You I am Praying*, but Mr. Roberts stopped the singing. 'It is too terrible to sing here,' was his remark. Similar scenes were witnessed also at the evening meeting."

Hon. Lloyd-George, a leading Baptist member of Parliament from Wales, "has instanced a case in which a man had told him that wagon loads of barrels of beer were carried back to Carnarvon because the publicans (saloons) could not sell them."

SEVENTY THOUSAND CONVERSIONS

It is easy to count the conversions in the Welsh revival, for when a surrender is made, the singing and praying stop, and a clerk appointed for the purpose takes down his name and address. It is wonderful, too, that nearly all of the converts forthwith join the churches and seek baptism. The latest report puts the number of converts at 70,000. "Last week an addition has been reported of twenty-one places to the revival area, and of about 18,000 to the number of converts."

THE ATONEMENT IN THE WELSH REVIVAL

What seems to me to lie at the heart of this revival in Wales is the unveiling of the cross, and the rediscovery of the power of intercessory prayer. These two facts place it at once in the true perspective, and show its relation to similar movements in other days. In the unveiling of the cross, there is an interchanging sense of grief and joy—*Did E'er such Love and Sorrow Meet?*

The most effective hymns of the present revival are in the key either of the sufferings of Jesus in the Garden and on Calvary, or of the gracious wonder of His atoning love. The thought of "the cold, unquiet night," of "His moanings at midnight outpoured," of His going to the hill and giving Himself to be nailed, willingly—this thought has, in the warm, dewy atmosphere of the last few weeks, become a present scene, with inexpressible personal significance, *Who Loved **Me**, and Gave Himself for **Me***. The other hymnal note is an exclamation of ever-fresh surprise at the vastness and triumph of love— vast as flowing oceans, resistless as mighty floods. There is no *dies irae* (*Latin* for day of judgement or day of wrath. Ed.) to terrify, but a *dies caritatis* (This expression is more obscure, but probably means day of charity. Ed.) to win its way as summer through a waiting wood. Sin—or at least vice—is seldom denounced: and yet the horror of a wicked past was never more real than it has been the last few weeks. It has stood out in black tempestuous relief, from the sad but redeeming glory in the face of Jesus Christ.

The British Weekly

COMMENTS ON THE REVIVAL

Notice some features, which also will mark the coming great revival here! It springs up among the poor and lowly. It is not worked up by the so-called "leaders." It does not depend on machinery and ecclesiastical manipulation. It is carried on *by the Holy Ghost!*

The evangelist is not a scholar, higher critic, college man; Roberts is a poor, illiterate boy out of the mines, with a bare common school education. He gives God all the glory! keeps in the *Spirit!* does not hinder *Him!* does not frustrate the *grace* of *God.* "Not many wise, not many mighty are called, but God hath chosen the weak things, yea the base things . . . that no flesh should glory in His presence!" (1 Corinthians 1:26, 29).

The people run the meetings, have full swing, are not bossed by a spiritual martinet, come early, stay late, weep and shout, pray and sing, go from house to house in love bearing precious seed—all at it! always at it! Formality is excluded! No big paid choirs! No pipe organs to entertain! Jesus is enough! Joy in every heart! Everybody prays, prays through, gets to God; gets the "Witness of the Spirit" for himself; no one tells them, when they are saved; they get it from headquarters. Hallelujah to God! The crowd comes; all classes; dirt, rags, poverty, they are all there to meet God! to see Jesus! Forms, ceremonies, images, evangelical tricks of the trade; long, tedious and dry sermons are not; they are *abolished* by the Holy Ghost! The Comforter has come! God has heard the cry of the masses—the poor, downtrodden, drunken masses, the robbed and crushed masses, tricked by priests, plundered by monopolies, deceived by bishops, fooled by their Pharisees, and misled by their guides, at last, the people have turned to *God. And He has heard their cry!* The papers follow—not lead—the revival. The masses have turned away from all else, and are finding help in God. He is sweeping away the refuge of lies, the formalism, hypocrisy, Phariseeism, as he did slavery after *He* started the great awakening of 1857. It is now nearly fifty years since that great work "broke out" among the masses, and swept away *slavery,* in spite of the formalists, Pharisees, senators, secesh, etc., etc. Our year of Jubilee is due in 1906—just forty-nine years after that one. The masses in this country are coming to the end of all help from laws, legislatures, labor unions, committees, higher critics, forward movements, holiness associations, churches, creeds, evangelists, missions, societies, and all that dead and useless junk heap of machinery. They will soon turn to God as all they have left. In 1857 the revival and a *panic* of awful financial distress came together. Their mammon god failed them. Trusts robbed them. Presidents and leaders like Pierce, Buchanan, Filmore, Webster, Clay, compromised sin, as their class are doing today, and went down in disgrace before the storm. As these bishops and presidents; and trusts, and rum legislatures will in this gathering storm under the wrath of *God!* Under the contempt of an awakened people, crying to *God* for help. We are having a foretaste of it. The mighty tidal wave of holy power is coming. But the big, great, wise, money bishops, leaders, colleges, will *not be in it! It will be God, and God only!*

The Life-Line

CALL TO PRAYER AND LEAGUE OF INTERCESSION
THE REVIVAL IS SPREADING

The wonderful revival which seems to have started in Wales has leaped the bounds of the old principality, and is now extending to different parts of England, and bids fair to spread over the British Isles. The work has been given a strong impetus in London by the great union meetings recently begun by Messrs. Torrey and Alexander. The great Central Hall that will seat 12,000 persons, is daily packed, so that, thousands are turned away. As a consequence other doors are opened and scores of prominent ministers and evangelists are pressing the work in all sections of the city.

The president of the English Wesleyan Conference has issued a circular letter to the Methodist people throughout the United Kingdom, calling them to special prayer and endeavor for the promotion of the revival. He says, "Judging from the evidence which has reached me, I cannot but conclude that the Welsh revival is a gracious work of God. It is not of man's getting up, but of God's sending down. It is idle to attribute such a movement to the 'power of personality when animated by an intense and conscious prepossession,' to 'animal magnetic excitement,' or to the mere 'enthusiasm of humanity.' Such explanations may satisfy those who have resolved to recognize the supernatural in nothing, but no sober, reverent thinker can accept them. The obscure and lowly origin of the work, its remarkable spontaneity and uniqueness, the humble but fearless agent, the progress of the work even in his absence, the triumphant power with which it sweeps obstacles from its path, and, above all, the great spiritual and moral results it has achieved, convince me that the finger of God is in it. High excitement may accompany it, and in some cases regrettable extravagances may occur, but these are accidents only, not essential elements of the movement. Calm and competent witnesses tell us that there is much more than emotion, that the depths of men's souls are moved, and God is a reality to all. When all the churches are roused into exultant life; when gamblers, drunkards, blasphemers, and even infidels, are reformed, and confess Christ with tears; when the converts hasten to pay their debts and publicly renounce their long-cherished vices, when the bitterness of estrangement melts, and the changed heart cries, 'I forgive them, and I hope they will forgive me,' and with tears the old friendship is renewed; when the movement surprises everybody and carries everything before it like a mighty wave of a great storm; when 30,000 souls have been rescued from sin; and when the Holy Spirit is thankfully recognized as the source of power and blessing, these are, in my judgment, the notes of a genuine, God-sent revival. No mere upheaval of public opinion, no wild burst of Welsh excitement, can account for the facts. No power but the Spirit of Pentecost can produce them. Let us rejoice to own His work, and give Him grateful praise.

"The attitude of our church, then, should be warmly sympathetic. It is a movement after our own heart, and in some respects like a repetition of past periods of our history. Methodism was born in a revival; it cherishes the revival spirit still. The duty of the hour, therefore, it seems to me, is to pray and prepare for the revival to visit our societies throughout the land. 'Will it extend through England?' men are asking. And one has answered, I think rightly, 'It depends upon England itself.' Yes, if we are ready, eager for the blessing, willing to welcome it, though it may reach us in unconventional forms, what should hinder us from receiving the mighty baptism? Given the necessary conditions, the Spirit will descend. Let us be ready to catch the fire."

Since the above letter was issued, it is reported through English papers that the number of conversions in Wales has reached 70,000, and with the work now in progress in England, it is probable by this time that it has reached 100,000. So greatly has the interest increased in England that "A League of Intercession" has been spontaneously instituted, and ministers and laymen of greatest prominence in all the churches are earnestly endorsing it. It started by the following letter:

A League of Intercession

"*Dear Friend:* The reports given in the daily papers from credible witnesses of the wonderful work of God now spreading over many parts of Wales, and the unmistakable evidences of its genuineness, are creating in the hearts of good people a great longing that the revival shall spread into England.

"Knowing of only one way by which so desirable an end can be obtained, namely, by united and earnest prayer, it has been borne in upon me that we might at once institute 'A League of Intercession' for this definite purpose, with these very simple conditions:

"*First.* That those who join the League do all in their power to spread information about the revival, and so help to fan the flame.

"*Second.* That each will try to get others to join the League, and so become a center of influence.

"*Third.* That each day all with one accord shall unite in earnest and importunate prayer that God will graciously send down upon the churches of this country the baptism of the Holy Spirit in renewing and reviving power.

"The promise made in Ezekiel 36:37 is specially applicable to our present need, 'Thus saith the Lord God, I will yet be inquired of by the house of Israel to do it for them. I will increase them with men like a flock.'

"Also in 1 John 5:14, 15, 'And this is the confidence that we have in Him, that if we ask anything according to His will, He heareth us, and if we know that He heareth us, whatsoever we ask we know that we have the petitions that we desired of Him.'

"In the first instance, I am writing this letter to a few who, I believe, are in full sympathy with such a movement. I have no wish to multiply committees or organizations, we have enough of these already, but that, in the quiet of our closets, we should besiege the throne, of grace on this one behalf.

"For my own encouragement, and as a guide to further action, will you kindly give me your assent in writing that you will join this 'League of Intercession,' and comply with its conditions I am yours very sincerely,

Thomas Walker
Southfield, Bolton"

This letter is being published in leaflet form, and scattered broadcast over the land.

We are quite sure that our readers will unite with us and our brethren across the water in this great League in earnestly praying that the revival will not only cover the British Isles, but may bound across the ocean and set America on fire. "The set time to favor Zion seems to have come, for her servants take pleasure in her stones and favor the dust thereof.

Way of Faith

STATEMENT OF LADY HENRY SOMERSET

Contrasting the Wales revival with another where she found less manifestation of the Spirit's presence and power, Lady Henry Somerset says:

Lady Henry Somerset

"But the impression produced on my mind may have been possibly heightened by the contrast presented by the wonderfully vivid realization of the simple work of the Spirit which has been blowing like the divine breath through the valleys of South Wales.

"There organization has been unknown, money has been unsought, newspaper puffs (flattery, promotion. Ed.) nonexistent; indeed, the revivalist has still to be found. True it is that the figure of Evan Roberts stands out strongly, and yet the revival is independent of him.

"He is the voice crying in the wilderness, 'Make ready the way,' but unquestionably the One that comes is the Unseen Presence of the Spirit of God. There is no order of service, no set choir, only bursts of wonderful Welsh melody, no hymn books—the words are written in the hearts of the worshipers. The little whitewashed chapels resound with song, song exquisite in its harmony, solemn as death, and yet jubilant as a choir of angels. Then stillness, prayers, soft sobbing from broken hearts, confession, profession, all the wonderful gamut of the soul's experience, but all spontaneous, with no settled effect, only the greatest effect of all, the reality of human need and divine power.

"What wonder Wales has been shaken as never before since the great religious revival a century and a half ago! What wonder the drink shops are empty, that at the assizes (courts of law. Ed.) there has been no crime!

"Everywhere as you move about you feel a great hush as though Christ walked over the mountains and into the mining towns and out through the valleys among the sons and daughters of toil, whose eyes have been opened to see Him as He came to them by the way."

Skeptics Convicted and Converted

The Rev. T. Ferrier Hutme, writing to the *London Methodist Times,* gives an interesting narrative of the triumph of the Holy Spirit over defiant skepticism in one town in Wales.

Referring to the early days of the revival, he says: "At that time Trecynon could boast of a so-called Ethical Society, composed of certain agnostics and atheists of various shades of unbelief, but chiefly out and out skeptics. They were avowed socialists and avowed materialists, and some of them were far advanced in their anti-Christian views before they received the welcome encouragement afforded to such men in these days by Haeckel and Blatchford and the *Clarion.*

The most noted of these characters was Tom Hughes, a man of forty, vivacious and witty, and a good singer. He could hear the singing in the chapel from his own house on the Sunday Evan Roberts came, and it was his own love of good music, along with the magnificent rendering by the entire congregation of those glorious Welsh songs, that was used by the Spirit to draw him. On Monday, Tuesday, and Wednesday he came, and stood in the lobby only, but On Thursday he ventured inside, longing to "touch the hem of His garment."

At 11 P.M. he left the chapel, and went home. His wife saw at a glance that a change had come over him, and that he was in great distress. He went to his little parlor, and took down from his shelves one by one the books he had so prized as a member of the local Ethical Society, and flung them on the table. Then with great deliberation and with intense emotion he took up one at a time, tore it in pieces and made a bonfire of the whole lot in his own grate (fireplace. Ed.).

As the flames shot up the chimney, and the blaze increased, his wife said, "Tom! Tom! what's the matter! You've lost your balance. You'll put the place on fire!" "Nothing of the kind, my dear," he said. "The Master, who has kept us safe through all these years while these cursed books were under my roof, will certainly take care of us tonight while I am destroying them." Altogether they were worth a few pounds, and so keen was he on their utter destruction that he afterwards said, "As I was watching them I was under the impression that the angels of God were there blowing the bellows and fanning the flames for me."

The work of destruction over, he said, "Now I am going back to the chapel, to give myself up to Christ."

"Tom! Tom! do be cooler, and act like a reasonable man."

"No, no," he said, "I've been a so-called reasonable man long enough, and now I've lost my reason entirely, as people will tell you, and it's time I did."

By this time the house was all astir, and the six children, of ages from sixteen to six, had all turned out of bed to see what it was all about. And children always enjoy a big bonfire, and especially if the hour be late—the later the better.

"Tom, dear," said his wife, "instead of going back to chapel let us sing like we used to do in former days before you got those books." And once more Tom Hughes was "fetched" by singing, and he and his wife and children sat singing till three o'clock that morning.

Was there ever a more beautiful and affecting scene than this in the whole history of family religion? Here is "the church in the house" of Tom Hughes, and this is the opening service, and the little parlor is the family pew! As I write my heart cries, "Hallelujah!" but I suppose I must be hysterical, and that just makes me want to shout it louder.

Well, on Friday he went at the usual hour to his work in the pit, where he is an under-official. All knew there was a change in him, and the four officials held a prayer meeting for him to ask that the change might be complete. In the evening the news spread through the little town like wildfire, "Tom Hughes is a captive for Christ!" And when halfway through the evening service his presence was recognized by the congregation, their jubilation was indescribable and their *Diolch Iddos* rang through the building again and again.

When he went to work on Saturday morning one said to him, "Tom, bach, (This is a term of endearment derived from "live as a bachelor." As an expression of affection, it meant "little one" or "young one," but was not age exclusive. Ed.) you are a converted man at last—welcome to Brynseion; your old chapel. The doors will be wide open to receive you back." He instantly replied with his well-known sprightliness, that has always helped to make him popular, "If the doors were not open, then I would come through the window. And if the windows were barred, then I would take a ladder and get on to the roof and come down through that, for come I will!"

On that Friday night scores were saved at both Ebenezer and Brynseion, and the services were what you would probably call tumultuous. Why? Because, as a man said at Cefu, near Merthyr, "Lord, we have generally had to wait a long time, but in these days we thank Thee Thou art sending us answers per return!"

And now I must tell of two or three more speedy answers. Saturday morning these chapels were packed again for prayer at 9:30, when Evan Lewis, a young man of thirty-two, another member of the Ethical Society, was converted—a fine young fellow of a high order. On Sunday, November 20, it was communion at Ebenezer Independent Chapel, and Evan Lewis got up and said in tones and gestures that revealed the all-consuming passion of his newborn soul, "Oh, do come to Jesus! If you only had just one such glance at Him as I had yesterday, not one of you could resist His appeal to come."

Tom Williams, also about thirty-two, and a member of the same clique, was up in the gallery when Evan Lewis spoke, and noticed how his words moved the whole assembly. Looking over the gallery, he saw below W. H. Davis, about thirty, who was the secretary of this Ethical Society. It occurred to him that he would go and ask the secretary there and then an important question, for he felt he was himself being rather shaken, and could hardly understand it.

So he set off to ask Davis, "What is the real philosophy of this strange influence that is coming over one and all in these meetings?"

Just as he got to the end of the gallery and was about to turn to get outside, he felt as if he was being crushed by an overwhelming power. He was as a man torn and twisted in every fiber of his being, and with all the force of which he was capable he resisted and "kicked back." The struggle was terrific, and the goad only pierced him more deeply. Just as he opened the door at the top of the stairs, he could stand it no longer, and cried, "Oh, infidel, infidel that I am! A second Saul of Tarsus, a blasphemer, and lo, He can twist me like a towel, and do with me as He wills!" Before he got downstairs he surrendered all; and then God, and not the secretary of the Ethical Society, answered his question, and explained the philosophy of it all to his utmost satisfaction. Isa. 1:18, "Come, now, and let us end our reasoning, saith the Lord. Though your sins be as scarlet they shall be as white as snow, and though they be red like crimson, they shall be as wool." It is all there.

The secretary that night followed Evan Lewis, whose mind he was persuaded was unhinged, and said, "Evan, come with me I want to chat privately with you." He raised his hand and gently pushed him aside, at which the secretary angrily assumed a fighting attitude, and raised his hand and clenched his fist as if to strike him. At that very moment another came up from behind and said, "If you dare aim a blow at Evan you'll be sorry for it. I'll see to that. I'll come with you, and debate instead, and just let Evan calm down. But I must go into my house first, and ask guidance and get my orders, and then I'll be with you."

He went and spent a little time in prayer, and then came out and said, "Now I'm ready for you." But by this time the secretary of the Ethical Society discovered that he himself was not, and declined the challenge, saying, "I'm not in a fit state myself to debate tonight."

That debate has not yet come off, for something else has happened to make it quite unnecessary. The secretary himself has been converted, and now the four most prominent men of that secular clique have definitely come over to the side of Jesus Christ, and are daily witnessing for Him. During the last three months the gracious work has been going on in all six chapels situated in Trecynon, and some 500 converts have been enrolled.

Far-Reaching Influence of Welsh Revival

From the reports to hand from South Wales, it is certain that there is no waning in the flame of the revival, but a steady extension of the fire northwards, with indications of religious awakenings in other parts of the country.

Indeed, it would appear that the world is ready for another mighty spiritual birth, which may prove a second Reformation. General Booth sends word that there is a quickening of religious life wherever he goes, and France, Holland, Denmark, Sweden, and Norway are, like England and the States, full of the expectation of a Divine springtime. Even London

William Booth

is mildly stirred, and the curious attitude of the halfpenny press to the Torrey-Alexander mission, and its persistent treatment of the mission as a revival, is not without meaning. It at least shows that religion is considered sufficiently important to notice.

The longer the revival in Wales lasts, says a religious writer—and there is, up to the present no indication of waning influence—the more apparent is it that its keynote is of a social and altruistic nature, and that, in this respect, it differs from those which have preceded it when the doctrine preached was one almost exclusively of faith rather than works.

Gipsy Smith, the well-known evangelist, in an interview in the course of which he was asked to account for the revival, said, "For a long time there has been a good deal of faithful ministry and faithful preaching going on in our midst. I have had a fair chance of judging, for I have seen many changes since I became an evangelist, but I have never found in my life so much faithful preaching and honest desire to see the church of God revived, on the part of the ministers, as at the present time. It is only fair to those who do the work on the spot to say that, for it is they who make it possible for us evangelists to come in and do the reaping. That means that faithful preaching in the pulpit has made people think in the pew; and caused people to pray."

Nearly a dozen students belonging to the (United Free) New College, along with two from the Divinity Hall of Edinburgh University, took advantage of the monthly holiday at the beginning of this week to spend a day or two in Wales and see something of the revival there.

All signs indicate that the revival is to be a universal, not a local movement. It is spreading rapidly in all parts of the country, like a fire along the prairie, and it is altogether interdenominational.

No weekly budget of news from Scotland, says the *Christian World,* would be at present representative that did not take notice of the growing and spreading anticipation of revival. From east and west, from north and south, from Edinburgh and Glasgow, from Aberdeen and the Border, comes the cry. The churches are all, or nearly all, preparing for something they are persuaded will come. But not only are they preparing, they are combining, and prayer meetings of separate and joint orders are being held.

The Bishop of Manchester, in his monthly letter to his clergy, commenting on revivals, says, "No doubt excitement has always attended them. The preaching of John the Baptist, and even of our Lord Himself, had manifestly a passing and exciting effect on multitudes, who eventually returned to their former ways, or even were hardened in sin. But the result was the foundation of the church and the beginning of new life for the world."

It is significant of the deep impression made by the Welsh Revival on widely separate schools of thought, that a sacerdotal organ like the *Church Times* should have taken up the cudgels (hitting with a stick. Ed.) in its favor in the face of certain harsh criticisms passed upon it, says the *Christian*.

Mr. Evan Roberts has promised to visit Liverpool at the beginning of March. Liverpool contains about 100,000 Welshmen, among whom the revival spirit is growing.

The *Goleuad,* the weekly organ of the Calvinistic Methodists, stated last week that one of the results of the revival in South Wales is the decision of a well-known solicitor (attorney. Ed.) to give up taking cases on behalf of brewers, and in doing this he is sacrificing £2,000 a year.

Dr. Torrey and Mr. Alexander have accepted an invitation in which Anglicans and Nonconformists have joined to conduct a mission in Sheffield during the month of September. The evening meetings are to be held in the Drill Hall, which is to be made to seat 5,000 people by the erection of temporary galleries. The meetings during the day are to be held in the Montgomery Hall.

The Bishop of Durham is probably the most wholehearted supporter on the bench of revivalism, and in a speech last week at Bishopwearmouth he so far uplifted the veil of secrecy as to what passed at the last Larabeth meeting as to say that bishop after bishop expressed a hope that the blessings which had unquestionably come to Wales should be extended to England. One of the wisest and most statesmanlike of English prelates said that it was clearly the work of the Holy Ghost.

The energy of the religious revival has at last manifested itself in the North, says a correspondent of the *Sabbath School Chronicle*. Many of us looked for first manifestations in Liverpool, the new metropolis of the principality, as it is termed, but, passing by this city, the stream of influence has caught the busy city of Leeds. Here, as I write, a revival is in progress.

Belfast Witness

SOUL TRAVAIL:
THE GROUNDWORK OF REVIVAL
BURDENS OF PRAYER

While Jesus is making intercession at the right hand of God, the Holy Spirit on the earth is praying through the hearts of those in whom He dwells. The human spirit is the vehicle through which the Holy Ghost pours His deep, divine yearnings, and in the same proportion that He widens and fills our souls, will He breathe into us these strong, sweet, melting intercessions, which are according to the will of the Father.

It is an infinite honor for the Spirit to put any burden of prayer on us, even when it is for our personal or family welfare; but when He draws us out into the priestly life of Christ, and puts in us unspeakable prayer for persons and objects that lie far beyond our personal or family interests, then it is in a higher sense praying in the Holy Ghost and alone for God's glory. The Spirit will divide and diversify His burdens of prayer according to the grace and gifts of each believer, calling some to pray in one direction and others in another, and He will put the pressure of prayer on and continue it, according to the soul's capacity, and its degree of willing cooperation with God in the prayer. A history of special burdens of prayer, as to their intensity and duration, would be amazing, especially if traced in connection with the answer that followed.

Soul Food

THE POWER OF PRAYER

All of the people who have been converted have been saved in answer to prayer. Every saint in glory is there in answer to somebody's prayer. On the other hand, all who have missed heaven have missed it through the neglect of prayer, and have gone down to the regions of eternal death from lack of prayer.

The powers of darkness are felt everywhere from lack of prayer. The devil has paralyzed to a great extent the church from lack of prayer. Many ministers have lost their power from lack of prayer. And many millions now throng the broad way to death from lack of prayer.

All of the great victories in the Christian church have taken place in answer to prevailing prayer. The Old Testament saints cried to God with an unearthly cry, and in answer to their prevailing prayer and favor with God they "subdued kingdoms, wrought righteousness, obtained promises, stopped the mouths of lions, quenched the violence of fire, escaped the edge of the sword, out of weakness were made strong, waxed valiant in fight, turned to flight the armies of the aliens." "Wherefore seeing we also (who read this article, as well as all others) are compassed about with so great a cloud of witnesses, let us lay aside every weight, and the sin which doth so easily beset us, and let us run with patience the race that is set before us; looking unto Jesus, the author and finisher of our faith" (Hebrews 12:1, 2).

What made Knox, Whitefield, Bunyan, Alleine, Abbott, Clowes, Finney, Carvosso, Muller, Wesley, Payson, and a host of others such burning and shining lights? What gave them such wonderful power over the people, such power to cast out devils? We answer, prayer; long, persistent, uninterrupted, prevailing prayer was the secret of their power with God and men.

S. B. Shaw

INTERCESSORY PRAYER

The overheard closet supplication of George Whitefield was, "Give me souls, or take my soul!"

Alleine, it is said, was infinitely and insatiably greedy for the conversion of souls; and to this end he poured out his heart in prayer and preaching.

Matthew Henry said, "I would think it a greater happiness to gain one soul to Christ than mountains of silver and gold to myself."

Doddridge said, "I long for the conversion of souls more sensibly than for anything besides."

The deathbed testimony of the sainted Brown was, "Now after forty years preaching Christ, I think

I would rather beg my bread all the laboring days of the week for the opportunity of publishing the gospel on the Sabbath than without such a privilege to enjoy the richest possessions on earth."

John Welsh, often in the coldest winter nights arising for prayer, was found weeping on the ground and wrestling with the Lord on account of his people. When pressed for an explanation of his distress, he said, "I have the souls of three thousand to answer for, while I know not how it is with them."

Ralph Wailer wrote, "My greatest desire is for the salvation of sinners. Oh, for souls! souls! the salvation of souls! Oh, could I always live for eternity, preach for eternity, pray for eternity, and speak for eternity! I want to lose sight of man, and see God only." Two days before his death he said, "At Liverpool and Boston I appropriated one hour each day to pray for souls, and frequently spent the time prostrate on my study floor; in addition to which I held night vigils, arising to pray each night at 12 o'clock. I do not say it to boast, but it appears plain to me that the secret of success in the conversion of souls is prayer."

Brainerd could say of himself, "I cared not where I lived, or what hardships I went through, so that I could but gain souls for Christ. All my desire was for the conversion of the heathen, and all my hope was in *God.*"

The Consecrated Life

SOUL-TRAVAIL

Deep, spiritual revivals come through soul-travail. "For as soon as Zion travailed, she brought forth her children." Isa. 66:8. Paul, being in great distress over some who had given great promise of piety and usefulness, said, "My little children, of whom I am again in travail until Christ be formed in you." Gal. 4:19. All successful revivalists and great soul-winners bear testimony to the necessity of soul-travail as a condition of success. The experience of Evan Roberts along this line is very conspicuous.

A reporter of the *Evening Express,* Cardiff, Wales, gives a description of the scene which occurred in Ramoth Chapel, Hirwain, during the soul-travail of Evan Roberts, for such it really was:

"No such extraordinary scene has yet been witnessed during the course of the revival. It was an ordeal as dreadful as that through which the young revivalist passed at Blaenanerch, when he got the Spirit's baptism which sent him on his great mission. I talked on Friday and Saturday to two of the leading ministers of the Calvinistic Methodist Church in Wales, who were on either side of him in the pulpit when it occurred. No words can depict the awfulness of Evan Roberts' agony they say. He clutched the Bible nervously, turned over its pages hurriedly, and then suddenly his face became distorted with pain. He fought against manifesting the emotion that convulsed every fiber of his being, and exclaimed despairingly in an undertone which those standing near him distinctly heard, 'O Lord, do stay Thy hand. I can endure this no longer.' The next moment he was on the pulpit floor, and there he lay prostrate for nearly a quarter of an hour. He was concealed from the view of the congregation by those standing around him, but his sobs rang through the building, and the "Oh! oh! oh!" repeated over and over again in varied tones, were heart-piercing in the extreme. When he recovered

himself and emerged from the ordeal and sat down,
these two ministers (whom I saw in different places,
one on Friday and the other on Saturday) told me
his countenance was well-nigh transfigured and
was quite angelic in its calmness and repose, and
they both heard him exclaim peacefully, 'O for the
strength of body to bear this weight of glory!' He
subsequently told them that he was sure God had
for some days previously been building up his body
to stand the intense strain of the ordeal in which he
had, in a most realistic sense, been partaker of
Christ's sufferings. He himself believes that it is by such
an ordeal that God enables him to agonize for souls.
Attempts of course are made to account for this on
physical grounds, such as hysteria, overwork, intense
nervous exhaustion, and the like. But others who are
familiar with the experiences of David Brainerd and
other saintly revivalists of former days, and who know
how day by day this young man in private as well
as in public lives in fellowship with God that is inti-
mate and deep, interpret such an incident in the
light of those words, 'Ye shall indeed drink of My cup
and be baptized with the baptism that I am baptized with.'"

Way of Faith

FROM REPORT OF RECENT MEETING IN ARON VALLEY, WALES

In the afternoon there was remarkable power
in the meeting. At one time the whole congregation
almost simultaneously broke forth into an intense
outburst of prayer, scores of people praying with
great and inexpressible fervor. For about a quarter
of an hour this went on, Mr. Roberts remaining in a
prayerful attitude, and, like the people, engaged

in earnest supplication. Some were standing up with uplifted hands, and others were on their knees. Strong men were sobbing like children, and pretty well all the congregation were in tears. There was another wonderful meeting at night, and many decisions.

London Christian

THE TOKEN OF A GENERAL REVIVAL

The evidences of the coming of a general religious revival, which shall move the whole country from border to border, are accumulating. It is true that, at this season of the year, and in our own church particularly, there is always considerable evangelistic success, and many converts are gathered in. But there is something more this year. If the "breaking up" has not actually come, there is a presentiment of it, a powerful and confident expectation in many quarters. This is based partly on the good tidings from Wales and from the Torrey-Alexander meetings in London; on the reports from Denver, Kansas City, Los Angeles, Schenectady, and New York (particularly in Calvary Church). Here in Cincinnati earnest efforts are being made in St. Paul and in other churches with excellent promise, and there is concert of action among the denominations. In New York City all the pastors of the city are planning for united efforts and there, as here, days of fasting and prayer are being observed with the one great object in view.

This is indeed the one most significant and encouraging sign in the spiritual heavens—the burden which has seemingly been rolled onto all pastors and churches alike. We do not remember anything quite so universal, persistent, and solemnly pressing in recent years. There is a widespread conviction, which has taken firm hold upon the churches that the times are urgent, that man's need of a great spiritual quickening and empowering is supreme, that we have come to a climax-hour in our history when God must manifest Himself mightily in the salvation of men. This profound feeling is displayed in the sermons of all of our evangelical pulpits. All of our religious papers are discussing the question in every issue. Even the radicals among religious bodies have taken up the tremendous theme from their own point of view. The daily papers are quick to notice what is in the air. The other day one of New York's most sensational sheets came out with front-page headlines about the preparations for revival. The atmosphere is being surcharged with revival energy.

And this gathering conviction is not simply the expression of man's desire. It is God's Spirit making itself (Himself. Ed.) felt through the human soul with which He is in touch. Does it sometimes seem as though men were very earnest for the salvation of sinners, and as if they prayed and entreated the Almighty in vain for a demonstration of converting power? Does there sometimes seem to be what a recent writer has styled "the Divine indifference?" when "earnest men watch with dismay the immoralities around them, the orgies of lust and crime, the prosperity of villains, the grinding of the poor, and in their struggle against it they seem to get no help;" when, as Carlyle said in his spleen (anger. Ed.), "God sits in heaven, and does nothing!" Or when, as Faber describes not how it really is, but how "it looks:"

"He hides Himself so wondrously,
As though there were no God;
He is least seen when all the powers
Of ill are most abroad."

This is the natural feeling which often oppresses us in laboring for the higher morality and civic life against the activities of the devil and devilish men. We almost react sometimes, too, in our evangelistic ardor, when our prayers seem to bring no answer whatever, into a pessimistic mood which imagines that the universe is deaf, and that nobody even in heaven itself cares whether men are saved or not. But, as the author we just quoted says, this would be the most egregious (enormous. Ed.) of mistakes. It is only the personal that can help the personal. God's approach to us is by the indwelling of His Spirit within us and the expression of that Spirit through us. He incarnates His very soul and passion in us. "The developing sentiment of the moral community, the sentiment which protests against injustice and works for a better order, is simply His voice in the world. He speaks to man *through* man, and no other way. Our very impatience with the oppositions and the slow progress is but the rush of the stream of His life in the too-narrow channels of our limited nature. The revolt of our conscience against the low moral order is His battle cry for a better one.

This it seems to us, is admirably stated, and it applies to our zeal and frequent impatience in spiritual movements as well as in moral crusades. Our prayers are not returning to us fruitless. God is already manifesting Himself in the growing intensity of His people.

There is a conviction, becoming constantly weightier, that men have really gone on quite far enough in paying such exclusive attention to material things—in frenzied rush after pelf (riches. Ed.), place, and power, in "the mad race after the dollar"—and that it is quite high time that the concerns of the immortal soul had some little attention paid them. We say we think there is discernible a very distinct reaction in that direction.

Again, there is the outcry of a public aghast at a seeming "tidal wave of immorality" breaking over the land. On every hand political corruption is rife. Divorce and lax marriage relations, fornication, and adultery scandalize us. In great cities, like New York and Chicago, murders, suicides, and "holdups" crowd on each other's heels. The newspapers every morning are records of a carnival of crime.

Is it any wonder that people everywhere are crying out, "O Lord, how long? Shall there be no end to this? Is there no help? If a revival of religion will make things safer, more decent, more protective of property, of chastity, civic purity, honor, and human life, let us all join in praying for it and working for it tremendously, for it is frightfully needed!"

But our souls must be thoroughly cleansed before God can bring His best answer. Why do we want men converted? To swell the church record? To help on with the finances? That we may make a vainglorious report at conference? That the evangelist may advertise his "thousand souls saved" through his instrumentality?

It will only be as we have an unaffected passion for men themselves and for their own good and for bringing them to their Savior, which is free from all ulterior motives, free from corrupting, worldly dross— that God can use as His instruments in conversion and revival. May this simple and sincere sympathy, this highest form of humanitarianism and philanthropy fill the heart of the entire church of Christ!

Western Christian Advocate

REVIVAL

Revival is possible. Revival is needed. Revival, if wide enough and deep enough, will set back the strong tide of sin and corruption that is sweeping away the life of the nation, and give it new lease and power. It will clean out the halls of legislation, the courts of justice, and the executive offices of government. It will make men honest in private and in public.

One of the special marks of the revival in Wales was emptying the saloon. Revival will blow to atoms the saloon, the brothel, and the gambler's pit. The revival will make men pray right, and they will vote, plump (The idea seems to be that men will fall to the ground as they pray earnestly. Ed.), as they pray, and make no excuse for it. Hallelujah!

We can all see that there is room for revival in church and in state.

As the statement is above made, the revival is possible. Yet good people, and spiritual, say that it is not possible. It is said that because with great spiritual efforts the local revivals are small, and only a few are saved; and furthermore, the wicked are so hardened, and Jesus is coming very soon; therefore we must not expect that there can be a grand sweep of revival, which shall astonish the nations and frighten hell. But such talk paralyzes effort.

The larger local revivals in this country indicate God's willingness. Instance Schenectady. And instance Denver, in a state and a city, of great political corruption, with a plenty of wickedness; where for a day business was suspended, and the legislature got cool enough and interested enough, to adjourn to attend the meetings.

The great revival in Wales is a powerful indication that Christ is still on the mediatorial throne, expressly to reach sinners, big and little; and that the Holy Spirit is still engaged in His grand outpour business, which is for "all flesh."

But the proper human agencies are still required. Let them come into line. The revival, deep and general, is on its way!

The great personal requisites to revival are few. Yet they may be named tremendous.

The first is absolute clearness in saving experience. Here something real and worthy can be accomplished; for the new life has in possession those elements of the love of our Lord which stimulate the activities into the very intercession of the Man of Calvary.

But as a higher insurance of effectiveness, the heart must be clean. This is not only salvation, but full salvation; not only forgiveness of every sin, but cleansing from the original sin of the heart, and therewith the inflooding of the personal Holy Ghost. All doubt (unbelief, which is primal sin) gone. The relations with God natural, unrestrained, and perfect. Here the human spirit is docile and teachable. It is ready for all lesser yet worthy activities, and finds itself, when stationed and developed by practice and call, quite capable of large and untrammeled plans. Holiness as a universal element is able to expand the human spirit into the necessities of the world of mankind.

Providence, and study, and spiritual intuition—really the call of God—have their partnership in leading us to see the general wants of the church of God. Danger has its forecasts, and leads us to forefend the day of destruction.

The desolations of the world and of the church bring the disciple of deep devotion and faith to the storehouse of all effective remedy, *The Blood-Bought Mercy Seat.*

Prayer, the genuine cry to God, is the appointed method of access to God. God is greatly in favor of revival. And He is stirring up the sainthood to pray for what He thus favors.

"Prayer is appointed to convey
The blessings God designs to give."

He wants partnership in the work, and must have it. Who of us is ready to join the great Prayer Union for the oncoming of the wide, deep, and tremendous revival, which is sure to come, and which already is gilding the spiritual horizon with its glory? Who?

Great is the reward to those who wait on God, who meet the conditions, and quietly and firmly go forward in this work.

There are many indications of the inception and progress of the Circle of Prayer for revival. Let us note some of them:

The valuable literature on prayer has increased substantially within a few years. There are divinely called teachers of prayer. The philosophy, the use-fulness, and the necessity of prayer are becoming more widespread among the real people of God. Many are entering into its beauties.

The great Convocation for Prayer, started to pro-mote unity in the holiness work, is especially charged with the thought of prayer in the direction of Joel's prophecy and Pentecost's incipient fulfilling of it, that the Spirit is to be poured out upon "all flesh."

In January a call to prayer was issued—or for prayer and fasting—on February—signed by "nine-teen prominent clergymen and workers"—"in view of the increased spirit of worldliness in the churches," "the dearth of genuine conversions," etc., that God would "speedily revive His work in our land."

Christian Harvester

THE REVIVAL NEEDED

Is it not time to cry aloud and spare not, to lift up the voice like a trumpet, and show the people of God their transgressions, and the house of Jacob their sins? Surely the need beside which every other need sinks into insignificance is an old-time revival, a deep and widespread old-time revival.

We are no pessimists. We do not for a moment lose sight of the fact that the foundations of God stand sure. We do not for a moment question that God has His thousands that have not bowed the knee to the world, the flesh, or the devil, nor been swept from their mooring by the present floodtide of false teaching and doctrine. These unite in declaring that the only remedy for the evils we deplore is an old-time revival—

a revival brought about by the mighty working of the Spirit of God in awakening and quickening and saving power. O for a revival that will turn the professed people of God back from their idols of sin and worldliness to serve the true and living God—back from their "broken cisterns" to the "fountain of living waters." A revival in which the Word of God will be preached without compromise or apology in the power of the Holy Ghost sent down from heaven. A revival that will overthrow sin of every kind, popular as well as unpopular. A revival that will take every desire for worldly amusements and abolish every ungodly scheme for raising money for the support of the gospel. A revival that will sweep away the pride that prompts all worldly conformity and extravagance in dress and manner of life, and melt the millions of dollars worth of gold that is now used to adorn the body, into coin, and dedicate it to God for carrying the gospel to the heathen. A revival that will take the people out of their worldly clubs and societies and secret lodges and put them into the "secret place of the Most High," where they will "abide under the shadow of the Almighty" (Psalm 91:1).

A revival that will save the people of God from covetousness and love of the world and all uncleanness of spirit, mind, and body. A revival in which professors of religion will have their eyes opened to see and feel their responsibility for souls, and in which they will confess with broken hearts their former backslidings, their carelessness and in-difference, and in thousands of cases their actual transgressions of the moral law. A revival like a flood that will "sweep away the refuge of lies" and "overflow the hiding places" of all them that would hide away from the light of God's Spirit. A revival that will unearth and uncover every device of Satan for deceiving souls, whether found in the church or outside of it, "For the secret of the Lord is with them that fear Him; and He will show unto them His covenant" (Psalm 25:14). A revival that will make both the church and the world to realize the shortness of time and the importance of eternity. A revival in which judgment light will shine not only on the unsaved but in which God's people will see their duty and realize their opportunity as those that have lost sight of the things of time in the light of the coming judgment. A revival that will make heaven and hell, Calvary and the resurrection, salvation from sin, cleansing through the blood, and the gift of the Holy Ghost, living realities by the revelations of the Spirit in harmony with the Word. A revival in which the sinfulness of sin will be so revealed that instead of excusing and pleading for it, souls will turn from it in utter loathing, and cry out, "O wretched man that I am! Who shall deliver me from this body of death" (see Wesley's notes on Rom. 7:24), and refuse to find comfort in any thought of imputed righteousness as a covering for sin, but cry out for deliverance from every wrong affection and from every evil thought and desire, and rest not until the old man is crucified with Christ, and the very body of sin destroyed. A revival that will sweep away selfishness and narrowness and all sectarian spirit, and bring those that now spend their time in criticism of each other down on their faces together before the Lord, crying out for the salvation of lost souls.

A revival that like a tornado will sweep away all the old dried-up sermons, and all the cold formal prayers, and all the lifeless singing, and like a whirlwind will carry every one that comes in its path heavenward. A revival that will fill the hearts of saints with holy love, and so burden the hearts of God's ministers that the word of God will be like fire shut up in their bones. (See Jer. 20:9). A revival that will help the people to honor God with their substance, and so have their barns filled with plenty (See Prov. 3: 9, 10).

A revival that will open the windows of heaven by bringing all God's tithes into His storehouse. A revival that will so fill the saints with love that they will rejoice in the opportunity to give their tithe and money, and if needs be their very lives, for their brethren and for the salvation of a lost world. A revival in which the presence of God will be so revealed that multitudes will fall under the power of God and cry for mercy as they did on the day of Pentecost. A revival that has so much of Heaven and so much of God's glory in it that all the world, will be compelled to see and feel its mighty influence. A revival that will gloriously defeat the powers of darkness and hell and make earth and heaven ring with shouts of victory over a multitude of souls snatched from the eternal burnings and run for God and heaven—yea, a revival that will never need to be revived, but that will sweep on like a mighty wave of the sea that nothing can hinder, until time shall be no more!

For such a revival our heart cries out to God! For such a revival we are ready to watch and toil and pray. For such a revival we believe the blessed Holy Spirit is interceding in many hearts. Such a revival God is able and ready to give. But for this He must be inquired of by His people to do it for them (See Ezekiel 37).

May God grant it, not for our sakes, but for His own name's sake and for His own honor and glory! Amen and amen.

Old-Time Religion

THE WELSH REVIVAL

The Welsh revival has already taken its place as one of the great popular movements in the history of Wales. From the small village in Cardiganshire where it started about a year ago, it is sweeping throughout the principality and into England, casting down before it as it goes all barriers of sect and station in life, a phenomenon much more remarkable in England than in other countries. The daily press of every kind and creed have been devoting a large amount of space to the accounts, sympathetic or otherwise, of the wonders that have been taking place in small Welsh villages, some of which had never been heard of before by the majority of people. The English are looking on at their Welsh neighbors much in the same manner in which a chicken might watch a duck swim. There is some envy, a little contempt for an emotionalism foreign to their nature, and a final sense of consolation at being at least on terra firma. In religious circles there is a wistful gazing westward in hopes of catching somewhat of this power that is shaking society to its foundations and creating a new heaven and a new earth in bleak and desolate Welsh villages. It is one of those fierce fires that cast a nation into the melting pot and one can only ask, "What stamp will it leave on the Welsh nation?"

There is a theory that all social and moral advance made by humanity may be traced to religious revivals. There is no doubt that this is the case with the Welsh. In 1756 there was, practically speaking, no Welsh nation and no religion in Wales. The copies of the Bible in their language were used by the ignorant peasantry as charms to ward off the evil eye or keep disease from the cattle. A revival came, and the Bible was spread broadcast, and with Welsh hymns became the nucleus of the Welsh literature. In 1800 another revival created Nonconformity in the sturdy principality. Fifty-nine years later, a visit paid to his old home by Humphrey Jones, of the American Methodist Episcopal Church, resulted in a third religious upheaval. These have left a deep mark on the life of the people. They are saturated with religion and Bible knowledge. From it their music, their art, their drama draw inspiration. In summer it is no uncommon thing for nine or ten churches to join in singing festivals. The meetings take place on the mountainsides, and the valleys ring with music and the chanted eloquence of the Welsh preacher. There is probably no country in the world which has in working order so perfect a system of Bible teaching in Sunday schools. Part of the study includes a three-year course in the life of Christ. Every child passes three times through this until the highest grade is reached. In this grade the adult congregation is found, and it deals with the deep problems of theology. Even the amusements of the people are often Biblical in origin. A choral society of a church will give a performance of an oratorio, entitled _Joseph_, in which the hero, "Pharaoh," the chief butler and baker, and many other characters, appear in suitable costumes. At another time, "Paradise" will be the theme, and the "creation" and the "fall" will be depicted in similar manner.

Every Welshman is either a quarryman, a miner, or a farmer, and when one reads of mass meetings of such workers, one imagines black faces and soiled hands. But at these gatherings they present a conspicuously clean, quietly dressed assemblage of men and women, the only suggestion of the mine being visible is a curious blue mottling (marking. Ed.) like an irregular tattooing where coal splinters have struck and entered the skin. As a class they are intelligent looking with foreheads high and broad. The high cheekbones, the long, straight nose, the arched eyebrows and dark, deep-set eyes, contrive to give the audience an appearance greatly above one of the same social grade in England.

Ostensibly the revival began in February, 1904, in New Quay, in Cardiganshire, a southern county in Wales. But it was not till the autumn of that year that it attracted to it the man who is now the central figure of the movement. Evan Roberts is the grandson of a Waterloo veteran, the son of a working collier, and he was himself a collier until he went to college to be trained as a minister. His mother unites in an uncommon degree gentleness and spiritual enthusiasm. At once resolute, persuasive, humorous, and shy, Evan Roberts speaks with simplicity both in manner and in substance, and shrinks from publicity or mere curiosity. He speaks of God and the devil with the assurance not only of one who has had communication with them, but who has actually seen them. The devil grins at him in his garden, he goes back into the house, and when he returns Jesus Christ is there smiling at him. One of the most hopeful signs is his absolute refusal to assume any position of authority. All are doing the bidding of the Holy Spirit, and all are able to receive the holy commands. When begged to visit certain villages—and he is now being urged to go everywhere, even to London—he replies, "I will give you a message. I should like the people to believe. They wait for me. They should wait only for the Spirit. Some one said they are almost breaking their heart for me to go. Will they almost break their heart for the Holy Spirit? Then it must come down. What does the Word say? 'Ask and receive.' It is just that. 'Ask and ye shall receive.' That is the promise. Believe it. Don't wait for me. Some are talking of the share that this denomination or that has in the work. It is not denominational. In Loughor we had all denominations—Methodists, Churchmen, Congregationalists, Baptists, every one."

There are in this revival certain features common to all revivals. Gusts of emotion sweep across the people, and the whole congregation of sane men and women sob like children. A fresh influence is brought to bear upon them, and they burst into a hymn that becomes perhaps for the first time since its birth a perfect paean (triumphant song. Ed.) of praise and thankfulness, or a prayer. Once more it is the expression of one soul; the souls of many fused into one by that intense and common desire which can turn a crowd of well-dressed, usually self-controlled citizens into a revolutionary mob, or an ordinary church service into a revival meeting. It is natural that people who are not susceptible to occult experiences should decry them as madness, as a dangerous excess, an orgy of excitement bound to cause a corresponding rebound. The *Lancet*, one of the leading medical journals in the United Kingdom, takes up this attitude very strongly, and a brain specialist has written to the daily press, saying that he quite expects a large increase in lunacy in Wales. But even supposing this to be the result, it is only absolute materialism that can find such a condition of affairs more deplorable than indifference to spiritual things. For in Wales it is to people in this state that the revival has come as a whirlwind and a storm, purifying the whole atmosphere. These prosperous colliers and miners, despite their substratum (foundation. Ed.) of Bible education, have become absorbed in gambling, betting, drinking, and the attendant evils. Their sports have been so ruined by these forces that one of the amusing results of the revival has been that in the districts affected it is difficult to arrange football matches. Converted men have burned their football and boxing costumes, and have banded themselves into special missions to their comrades. "Coffee Cooler," who has lived to see his school of pugilistic (boxing. Ed.) art and science stormed by men and women imploring those inside to come out and be saved, says he has not received such treatment in heathen Africa. The innkeeper, who has hitherto dispensed water in small medicine bottles, expressive of her contempt for it as a beverage, is now resignedly selling tea to her customers. Creditors who had lapsed into despairing silence have had debts paid in full.

In one way the Welsh revival might be regarded as a triumph for Quakerism. There is no "order of service." That has been swept aside, and the meeting is left entirely to the guidance of the Holy Spirit. But the element that separates it from Quakerism is the large part played by song and the singing of hymns. The "Singing Sisters," as they are called, have done much to make the movement the rapid, vivid thing it is. Pent up feeling has found expression in hymn after hymn. The people are the rulers. A hymn is followed by a prayer, but if it is too long, a soul unable to repress its feelings any longer, starts another hymn. There is a moment's hesitation, then either the people choose the hymn or remain silent. Even speakers are thus interrupted, Evan Roberts himself submitting to the "musical closure" as a natural and right thing.

Practical measures are being taken to see to it that men and women who have broken from their past lives are helped to keep to their new resolutions. It is felt that the church must be ready to fill the place of all the interests that have been abandoned, to provide clubs for public houses, gymnasiums, clean football free from the taint of betting. What will grow from this is undoubtedly the "institutional church," with those social methods that have been carried out with such success in London by different churches, but of which Whitefield's Tabernacle, under Rev. Silvester Home, is at present the most advanced and complete.

London ministers and people from all parts of the country, and even from the continent of Europe, are visiting Wales to study conditions at the "storm center." Even skeptics leave full of amazement at what they have seen and heard, so powerful is the impression given that there is working among the people a power that can only be described, because of its results on the character and the moral tone of the villagers, as the Holy Spirit.

Douglas Shields
The World Today

Evan Roberts' Grave

The Complete Azusa Street Library

The Comforter Has Come!

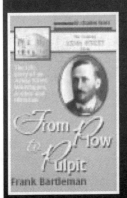

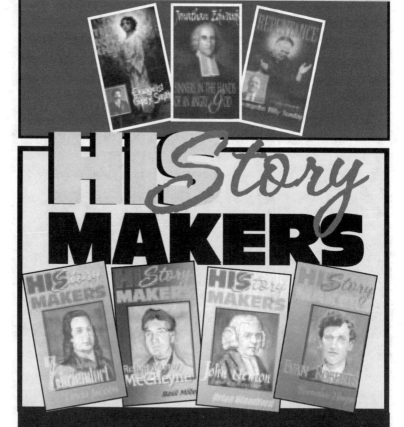

  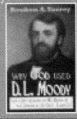 

azusa street NOW CONFERENCE

with **Dr. Larry Martin**

P.O. Box 36355 + Pensacola, Florida 32516

www.azusastreet.org

You can invite Dr. Larry Martin to teach on the life of Bishop Willam Seymour and the Azusa Street Revival at your church, conference or event. Dr. Martin, a missionary evangelist, is a leading authority on the historic revival and the editor and publisher of The Complete Azusa Street Library. He is also available for revivals, crusades and church services Please visit our websites or send us an email for more details:

drlarrymartin@azusastreet.org
www.drlarrymartin.org
www.azusastreet.org